Carnegie Commission on Higher Education
Sponsored Research Reports

A DEGREE AND WHAT ELSE?:
CORRELATES AND CONSEQUENCES
OF A COLLEGE EDUCATION
Stephen B. Withey, Jo Anne Coble, Gerald
Gurin, John P. Robinson, Burkhard
Strumpel, Elizabeth Keogh Taylor, and
Arthur C. Wolfe

INSTITUTIONS IN TRANSITION:
A PROFILE OF CHANGE IN HIGHER
EDUCATION
(INCORPORATING THE 1970 STATISTICAL
REPORT)
Harold L. Hodgkinson

EFFICIENCY IN LIBERAL EDUCATION:
A STUDY OF COMPARATIVE INSTRUCTIONAL
COSTS FOR DIFFERENT WAYS OF
ORGANIZING TEACHING-LEARNING IN A
LIBERAL ARTS COLLEGE
Howard R. Bowen and Gordon K. Douglass

CREDIT FOR COLLEGE.
PUBLIC POLICY FOR STUDENT LOANS
Robert W. Hartman

MODELS AND MAVERICKS:
A PROFILE OF PRIVATE LIBERAL ARTS
COLLEGES
Morris T. Keeton

BETWEEN TWO WORLDS:
A PROFILE OF NEGRO HIGHER EDUCATION
Frank Bowles and Frank A. DeCosta

BREAKING THE ACCESS BARRIERS:
A PROFILE OF TWO-YEAR COLLEGES
Leland L. Medsker and Dale Tillery

ANY PERSON, ANY STUDY:
AN ESSAY ON HIGHER EDUCATION IN THE
UNITED STATES
Eric Ashby

THE NEW DEPRESSION IN HIGHER
EDUCATION:
A STUDY OF FINANCIAL CONDITIONS AT 41
COLLEGES AND UNIVERSITIES
Earl F. Cheit

FINANCING MEDICAL EDUCATION:
AN ANALYSIS OF ALTERNATIVE POLICIES
AND MECHANISMS
Rashi Fein and Gerald I. Weber

HIGHER EDUCATION IN NINE COUNTRIES:
A COMPARATIVE STUDY OF COLLEGES AND
UNIVERSITIES ABROAD
Barbara B. Burn, Philip G. Altbach, Clark Kerr,
and James A. Perkins

BRIDGES TO UNDERSTANDING:
INTERNATIONAL PROGRAMS OF AMERICAN
COLLEGES AND UNIVERSITIES
Irwin T. Sanders and Jennifer C. Ward

GRADUATE AND PROFESSIONAL EDUCATION,
1980:
A SURVEY OF INSTITUTIONAL PLANS
Lewis B. Mayhew

THE AMERICAN COLLEGE AND AMERICAN
CULTURE:
SOCIALIZATION AS A FUNCTION OF HIGHER
EDUCATION
Oscar and Mary F. Handlin

RECENT ALUMNI AND HIGHER EDUCATION:
A SURVEY OF COLLEGE GRADUATES
Joe L. Spaeth and Andrew M. Greeley

CHANGE IN EDUCATIONAL POLICY:
SELF-STUDIES IN SELECTED COLLEGES AND
UNIVERSITIES
Dwight R. Ladd

STATE OFFICIALS AND HIGHER EDUCATION: A SURVEY OF THE OPINIONS AND EXPECTATIONS OF POLICY MAKERS IN NINE STATES
Heinz Eulau and Harold Quinley

ACADEMIC DEGREE STRUCTURES: INNOVATIVE APPROACHES PRINCIPLES OF REFORM IN DEGREE STRUCTURES IN THE UNITED STATES
Stephen H. Spurr

COLLEGES OF THE FORGOTTEN AMERICANS: A PROFILE OF STATE COLLEGES AND REGIONAL UNIVERSITIES
E. Alden Dunham

FROM BACKWATER TO MAINSTREAM: A PROFILE OF CATHOLIC HIGHER EDUCATION
Andrew M. Greeley

THE ECONOMICS OF THE MAJOR PRIVATE UNIVERSITIES
William G. Bowen
(Out of print, but available from University Microfilms.)

THE FINANCE OF HIGHER EDUCATION
Howard R. Bowen
(Out of print, but available from University Microfilms.)

ALTERNATIVE METHODS OF FEDERAL FUNDING FOR HIGHER EDUCATION
Ron Wolk

INVENTORY OF CURRENT RESEARCH ON HIGHER EDUCATION 1968
Dale M. Heckman and Warren Bryan Martin

The following reprints and technical reports are available from the Carnegie Commission on Higher Education, 1947 Center Street, Berkeley, California 94704.

RESOURCE USE IN HIGHER EDUCATION: TRENDS IN OUTPUT AND INPUTS, 1930–1967, *by June O'Neill, published by Carnegie Commission, Berkeley, 1971 ($5.75).*

ACCELERATED PROGRAM OF MEDICAL EDUCATION, *by Mark S. Blumberg, reprinted from* JOURNAL OF MEDICAL EDUCATION, *vol. 46, no. 8, August 1971.*

SCIENTIFIC MANPOWER FOR 1970–1985, *by Allan M. Cartter, reprinted from* SCIENCE, *vol. 172, no. 3979, pp. 132–140, April 9, 1971.*

A NEW METHOD OF MEASURING STATES' HIGHER EDUCATION BURDEN, *by Neil Timm, reprinted from* THE JOURNAL OF HIGHER EDUCATION, *vol. 42, no. 1, pp. 27–33, January 1971.*

REGENT WATCHING, *by Earl F. Cheit, reprinted from* AGB REPORTS, *vol. 13, pp. 4–13, no. 6, March 1971.*

WHAT HAPPENS TO COLLEGE GENERATIONS POLITICALLY?, *by Seymour M. Lipset and Everett C. Ladd, Jr., reprinted from* THE PUBLIC INTEREST, *no. 24, Summer 1971.*

AMERICAN SOCIAL SCIENTISTS AND THE GROWTH OF CAMPUS POLITICAL ACTIVISM IN THE 1960s, *by Everett C. Ladd, Jr., and Seymour M. Lipset, reprinted from* SOCIAL SCIENCES INFORMATION, *vol. 10, no. 2, April 1971.*

THE POLITICS OF AMERICAN POLITICAL SCIENTISTS, *by Everett C. Ladd, Jr., and Seymour M. Lipset, reprinted from* PS, *vol. 4, no. 2, Spring 1971.*

THE DIVIDED PROFESSORIATE, by Seymour M. Lipset and Everett C. Ladd, Jr., reprinted from CHANGE, vol. 3, no. 3, pp. 54–60, May 1971.

JEWISH AND GENTILE ACADEMICS IN THE UNITED STATES: ACHIEVEMENTS, CULTURES AND POLITICS, by Seymour M. Lipset and Everett C. Ladd, Jr., reprinted from AMERICAN JEWISH YEAR BOOK, 1971.

THE UNHOLY ALLIANCE AGAINST THE CAMPUS, by Kenneth Keniston and Michael Lerner, reprinted from NEW YORK TIMES MAGAZINE, November 8, 1970 .

PRECARIOUS PROFESSORS: NEW PATTERNS OF REPRESENTATION, by Joseph W. Garbarino, reprinted from INDUSTRIAL RELATIONS, vol. 10, no. 1, February 1971.

. . . AND WHAT PROFESSORS THINK: ABOUT STUDENT PROTEST AND MANNERS, MORALS, POLITICS, AND CHAOS ON THE CAMPUS, by Seymour Martin Lipset and Everett Carll Ladd, Jr., reprinted from PSYCHOLOGY TODAY, November 1970. (Out of print.)*

DEMAND AND SUPPLY IN U.S. HIGHER EDUCATION: A PROGRESS REPORT, by Roy Radner and Leonard S. Miller, reprinted from AMERICAN ECONOMIC REVIEW. May 1970. (Out of print.)*

RESOURCES FOR HIGHER EDUCATION: AN ECONOMIST'S VIEW, by Theodore W. Schultz, reprinted from JOURNAL OF POLITICAL ECONOMY, vol. 76, no. 3, University of Chicago, May/June 1968. (Out of print.)*

INDUSTRIAL RELATIONS AND UNIVERSITY RELATIONS, by Clark Kerr, reprinted from PROCEEDINGS OF THE 21ST ANNUAL WINTER MEETING OF THE INDUSTRIAL RELATIONS RESEARCH ASSOCIATION, pp. 15–25. (Out of print.)*

NEW CHALLENGES TO THE COLLEGE AND UNIVERSITY, by Clark Kerr, reprinted from Kermit Gordon (ed.), AGENDA FOR THE NATION, The Brookings Institution, Washington, D.C., 1968. (Out of print.)*

PRESIDENTIAL DISCONTENT, by Clark Kerr, reprinted from David C. Nichols (ed.), PERSPECTIVES ON CAMPUS TENSIONS: PAPERS PREPARED FOR THE SPECIAL COMMITTEE ON CAMPUS TENSIONS, American Council on Education, Washington, D.C., September 1970. (Out of print.)*

STUDENT PROTEST—AN INSTITUTIONAL AND NATIONAL PROFILE, by Harold Hodgkinson, reprinted from THE RECORD, vol. 71, no. 4, May 1970. (Out of print.)*

WHAT'S BUGGING THE STUDENTS?, by Kenneth Keniston, reprinted from EDUCATIONAL RECORD, American Council on Education, Washington, D.C., Spring 1970. (Out of print.)*

THE POLITICS OF ACADEMIA, by Seymour Martin Lipset, reprinted from David C. Nichols (ed.), PERSPECTIVES ON CAMPUS TENSIONS: PAPERS PREPARED FOR THE SPECIAL COMMITTEE ON CAMPUS TENSIONS, American Council on Education, Washington, D.C., September 1970. (Out of print.)*

*The Commission's stock of this reprint has been exhausted.

A Degree and What Else?

A Degree and What Else?

CORRELATES AND CONSEQUENCES

OF A COLLEGE EDUCATION

by Stephen B. Withey

Professor of Psychology and Program Director,
Institute for Social Research,
The University of Michigan

with chapters by

Jo Anne Coble, Gerald Gurin, John P. Robinson,
Burkhard Strumpel, Elizabeth Keogh Taylor, and Arthur C. Wolfe

7 2094

A Report Prepared for

The Carnegie Commission on Higher Education

MCGRAW-HILL BOOK COMPANY

New York   St. Louis   San Francisco   Düsseldorf
London   Sydney   Toronto   Mexico   Panama
Johannesburg   Kuala Lumpur   Montreal
New Delhi   Rio de Janeiro   Singapore

The Carnegie Commission on Higher Education,
1947 Center Street, Berkeley, California 94704,
has sponsored preparation of this report as
part of a continuing effort to present significant
information and issues for public discussion. The
views expressed are those of the authors.

A DEGREE AND WHAT ELSE?
Correlates and Consequences of a College Education

Library of Congress catalog card number 74-172034

123456789MAMM7987654321

07-010035-7

Contents

Foreword

The huge enrollments that fill and overflow America's colleges and universities constitute impressive evidence that our young men and women, and their parents, believe that going to college will make a beneficial difference in one's life. Testing that assumption systematically, however, proves to be difficult. The backgrounds of people who attend college vary and are bound to have some major influences on the ultimate findings of benefit studies. The circumstances of life after graduation may either reinforce or erode changes that take place during the college years and thus can produce significant distortions in research conclusions.

Despite the difficulties involved in determining the ways going to college changes men and women, scores of social scientists have made attempts. The objectives of such studies vary, but they all tend to contribute to our understanding of the general question: "What are the measurable changes and benefits that result from going to college?" At the request of the Carnegie Commission on Higher Education, Stephen Withey and his colleagues have made a comprehensive review of these earlier studies. Their findings are reported in this volume.

They conclude, among other things, that not only does going to college yield benefits, but every added year of postsecondary education yields additional impact and benefits. Those who embark on careers outside the home have better opportunities, more job satisfaction, and better working conditions. But the authors are not concerned only with economic-oriented change. They also are concerned with higher education's effect on life-style, use of mass media, and political behavior.

They warn us that the collection of data for effective measurement of impact is still incomplete and that the methods of such studies need further refinement. They also make the wise observation that the word *benefit* has meanings associated with specific points of time and with the experience and interests of specific groups of individuals. Since these meanings are constantly changing, the need for updating benefit studies is great. In the meantime, this report by Withey and his fellow authors provides a useful guide to the best knowledge available so far.

Their study clearly shows, on the data now available, that there are many plusses but also some minuses in college attendance from the point of view of the individual and society. Individuals who go to college tend to be:

- More "liberal" and tolerant in their attitudes toward and in their relations with other individuals and groups in society
- More satisfied with their jobs
- More highly paid and less subject to unemployment
- More thoughtful and deliberate in their consumer expenditures
- More likely to vote and to participate generally in community activities
- More informed about community, national, and world affairs

Women who go to college are more likely to work and also to have fewer children on the average. All these characterisitics may be viewed as being on the constructive side. But college attendance also gives greater accent to certain problems in society:

- To the prolongation of youth with its inherent tensions
- To the generational conflict between the more highly educated younger generation and the less educated older generation
- To the conflict within the younger generation between those who go to college and those who do not
- To the opposition between those who have more "liberal" and those who have more "conservative" points of view on social issues

One implication for the Republican party, in particular, is that college graduates tend not only to vote Republican more than nongraduates but also to be more "liberal"; the Republican party may be both aided in its numbers of adherents and changed in its general policy stance as a result.

All these apparent consequences and correlates should be viewed from the perspective that college attendance is but one of many influences on the lives of people, and not necessarily the most significant. It is also important to note that, while colleges differ from each other greatly, the data now available indicate—rather surprisingly—that it is the general impact of all colleges that matters more than the differential impacts of one type of college versus another type.

Yet it may be said, as a broad observation, that going to college—any college—does give to the individual a chance for a more satisfying life and to society the likelihood of a more effective community, even at the cost of intensifying certain inherent problems and cleavages in the postindustrial world. The hopes that Benjamin Franklin and Thomas Jefferson had so long ago for the contributions of education to American society have been largely realized. Their faith still remains well justified in modern circumstances.

Clark Kerr

Chairman
The Carnegie Commission
on Higher Education

June 1971

A Degree and What Else?

1. Problems in Assessing Impact

Stephen B. Withey

THE CHANG-
ING COLLEGE
AND ITS
STUDENTS Educational aspirations still outdistance achievement in the United States. A steadily increasing proportion of American youth aspires to some post-high school education; the figure now stands at about 80 percent of all high school seniors. Over two-thirds do enroll in some form of education after the twelfth grade, many in college. About one-half of high school seniors set college graduation as their goal. Not nearly that many reach it (Brim, Glass, Neulinger,& Firestone, 1969).

What for the student is at first a rather vague image of "college" becomes increasingly defined and realistic as the time approaches for applying, enrolling, and finally attending. What are the characteristics of people who attend college? What happens in the college experience? What are its consequences in adult life? What predictions might one make for the future?

Answers are not easy because college is an evolving, changing, varied, and complex social institution. The researcher interested in human behavior has divided his findings by educational attainment and often has found significant differences among the educational categories. But a closer look raises questions about the meaning and interpretation of the college category.

The roots of higher education in the United States are generally considered to date back to the writing of the Harvard charter. But in methods of instruction, students and faculty, goals and physical dimensions, the college of today bears little, if any, resemblance to the college of colonial times.

Higher education is no longer the privilege of a favored few, or even a right that one can choose to exercise. Rather, it is becoming obligatory, a requirement which must be met to achieve and maintain a "comfortable" standard of living. Increasingly, certification of competence to function adequately in a complex society, granted in the past for possession of a high school diploma, is not granted until an individual has a college degree. This has not gone unnoticed by those most directly affected: high school seniors. One study found that of the four out of ten high school seniors in 1965 who expressed no desire for a college education, about one-fourth planned to attend nevertheless. Of racial minority high school seniors, one-half expressed no interest in a college education; but one-half of these planned to enroll (Jaffe & Adams, 1969, p. 2).

Data on educational attainment of the population prior to 1870 are not available. But it is clear that graduation from college was a rarity. Since completion of high school is a major determinant of eligibility for college attendance, a rough idea of the number of persons eligible to attend college can be obtained by examining data on high school graduation. In 1870, 2 percent of the 17-year-old population graduated from high school (U.S. Bureau of the Census, 1960). Over three-fourths of the white population beyond age 65 enumerated in the 1940 Census (who would have graduated from high school immediately before the turn of the century) had gone no further than the eighth grade. Of the nonwhite members of this cohort 95 percent had completed eight years or less of schooling. Only 15 percent of whites had received some high school education; of these, a little more than half graduated from high school. Among nonwhites, 3.5 percent attended high school, and about one-third of the high school entrants graduated. About 15 percent of high school age students actually graduated from high school (Jaffe & Adams, 1969) in 1900.

In 1940 only 38 percent of the 25- to 29-year-olds were high school graduates. In 1969 about twice that proportion had finished high school. Among blacks alone, the rise in educational attainment is even more dramatic. In 1940 only 12 percent of black 25- to 29-year-olds had completed high school; but in 1969, 56 percent were high school graduates.

In 1870 fewer than 1 in 50 of the 18- to 21-year-olds was attending college (U.S. Bureau of the Census, 1960). In 1935, 10 in 50 whites and 5 in 50 nonwhites of high school age entered college. In 1960, about 20 in 50 of the 18- to 21-year-olds were going to college after high school—4 in 10 whites and 2 in 10 nonwhites of high school age (U.S. Bureau of the Census, 1960; Jaffe & Adams, 1969).

Almost half of all high school graduates now go to college. But almost half of all high school graduates went to college 50 years ago, although there was a slight drop during the depression years of the thirties. The proportion may be starting to increase. Although there is no increase among women (42 percent of 20- to 21-year-old, female, high school graduates have completed one year or more of college), the proportion of men who are high school graduates with one year or more of college has jumped from 49 percent among 22- to 24-year-olds to 58 percent among 20- to 21-year-olds (U.S. Dept. of Commerce, ser. P-20, 1969 & 1970).

The pool of potential college students has vastly expanded. The implication of available data is that, while college attendance in the late nineteenth and early twentieth centuries was limited to people of high socioeconomic status and relatively high ability, today's college entrants represent a much wider range of ability and social status. Consequently, we might expect the college retention rate to have decreased considerably. Instead, the proportion of college entrants who complete their education has remained at about 50 percent (Jaffe & Adams, 1969). That the overall college retention rate has not changed very much is a reflection of the changed nature of college education—the growth of existing institutions and establishment of new ones, altered methods of instruction, and different curricula.

In 1870, about 52,000 students were enrolled in institutions of higher education (a figure now exceeded in some single institutions). The total number of college graduates in the United States in 1940 was less than the approximately 7.5 million students now enrolled. Also, during the last three decades, the number of colleges and universities has almost tripled.

Colleges have become sprawling towns, some with tens of thousands of students. Some colleges have established several branches. Community colleges now serve local needs; two-year colleges serve the dual purpose of providing extended education for some, and acting as a feeder to four-year institutions. Colleges have increased their community services, and research activities have grown. College life has taken on new characteristics; for example, more students are now living with their parents, other relatives, or in their own households than in college housing; and the majority of them are already ahead of their parents in educational attainment.

The growth of community (or junior) colleges is regarded as one of the major responses to the increased demand for higher education. At least one researcher (Clark, 1960) sees junior colleges as an institutionalized "cooling-out" channel. According to this view, students who are unable or unwilling to enter four-year colleges and universities, or who try a four-year institution and cannot "make it," are not denied outright the opportunity of a college education. They have a channel for obtaining a degree, albeit an Associate of Arts degree rather than a bachelor's. Thus, "systematic discrepancy between aspiration" and achievement "is covered over and stress for the individual and the system is minimized" (Clark, 1960).

It is unfair to expect the typical college enrollee or graduate of today to be similar to his counterpart of a few decades ago. As colleges have changed, the mix of departments, curricula, students, organization, and purposes has shifted. Students have increased in number and changed in interests, abilities, and goals—as well as in sex, race, and socioeconomic status. There has also been change in what college graduates do with their education. The occupational and income mix continues to be slowly stirred by political, social, and economic forces. Most of this movement and change is, of course, only part of the change in society that makes new demands on its educational institutions as doors to opportunity are both closed and opened.

DIFFICULTIES IN ANALYSIS If it is difficult to compare the present with the past, it is equally hazardous to project into the future. One is tempted after studying the characteristics of college attenders and graduates to project these attributes into the future as descriptions of a growing sector of the population. But this must be done with caution. What was true for an admitted elite is not so applicable to a wider sector of society. What was true for a smaller core of institutions may not be so true for a larger group of increasingly varied colleges. What was true for the youth of one decade may not be so true for youth in a decade of different social, political, economic, and ethical conditions. Interpretations and projections need the advantage of insight into the dynamics and context for what is occurring. These insights are often not clear.

Morgan (1967) describes some of these pressures and problems:

In some recent work on change in the level of completed education between one generation and the next, we have looked at the possibility of extrapolating by using a distribution of transition probabilities between father and son over several generations of the future, to see what the distribution of education would look like three generations hence if the same pattern continued. Examination of this so-called Markov process shows that the average levels of education in the country will increase, but probably at a decreasing rate. Converting transition probabilities into a Markov process is tricky, of course, because people have different numbers of children, and the number of children may affect the transmission itself. Children of large families tend to get less education. By starting with a population of heads of spending units (most of the men in the population) and using the relation of their education to that of their fathers, one weighs the conditional probabilities by the number of sons to which they apply.

Such analyses are crucial because estimates of the future labor force, the demand for public support for education, and the possible shortage of teachers, all depend on the results of such projections. Similar long-term analyses of the participation of wives in the labor force can be devised using several alternative approaches. The more we know about the details of the present situation and its trends, the more intelligent these projections can be.

These types of projections—population size, labor-force shortages or surpluses, income redistribution, political majorities—are not attempted here. Instead the focus is on examining the research literature for indicators of characteristics that seem to accompany or become associated with educational attainment at the college and university level. But the reader should be wary in inferring causation from correlations and in leaping from simple statistical associations to judgments of significant economic, social, or political developments.

One should have reservations, too, about the accuracy of data obtained from reports by people with different educational backgrounds.[1] It is not surprising to find evidence that higher-educated respondents appear to be more efficient reporters than the less-well educated. Much self-reporting in surveys requires organizing ideas or opinions, retrieval of information from memory, and verbal facility. These are skills required of the person who succeeds at higher educational levels. They are part of the training associated with educational attainment.

In a study of the validity of reporting visits to physicians' offices (Cannell, Fowler, & Marquis, 1968), a significant improvement in reporting ability was found among higher-educated respondents (Table 1). Similar patterns are observed in reporting accuracy of chronic illnesses. A different pattern was found, however, in two separate studies of validity of reporting hospitalization. As Table 2 shows, the relationship of education and reporting may not be a simple linear one. Respondents who completed high school or

[1]The tables and text on reporting validity were prepared for this volume by Charles Cannell and Sally Robison.

TABLE 1
Validity of
reports of visits
to a physician
by educational
level

Education of respondent	Number of visits from records	Percent of visits not reported
0–8 years grade school	121	26
1–3 years high school	132	22
4 years high school	113	23
1 year or more college	33	9

SOURCE: Cannell, Fowler, & Marquis, 1968.

college are significantly better reporters than those who did not graduate. The hypothesis that persons who perform adequately in one role (student) may also be better performers in another (respondent) is suggested. Fowler (1965) presents evidence to support the hypothesis that the better educated are more efficient reporters. Table 3 shows that the educated gave fewer inadequate answers and that the interviewer used significantly more probes with the lower-educated groups in an attempt to stimulate adequate responses.

Better-educated respondents usually understand more about a survey and may therefore be more highly motivated to report accurately and completely. Cannell et al. (1968) found that while 29 percent of respondents with high school or higher education could not report who was conducting and sponsoring the survey, what the stated purposes were, and how the information was to be used, as many as 61 percent of respondents with less education were unable to report any of this material about a federal government national health survey. Further, there was a significantly high correlation between educational achievement and the respondent's knowledge of whether the interviewer wanted exact answers and not merely rough estimates.

Lansing, Ginsburg, & Braaten (1961), in a study of reporting of

TABLE 2
Validity of
reports of
hospitalization
by educational
level

Education of respondent	Number of hospitalizations from records	Percent not reported
Less than high school graduate	829	13
High school graduate	646	7
Some college	180	16
College graduate	155	5

SOURCE: Cannell, Fowler, & Marquis, 1968.

TABLE 3
*Adequacy of
responses to
questions by
educational
level (in percent)*

Number of answers inadequate to question objective	0–8 yr grade school	1–3 yr high school	4 yr high school	1 or more yr college
		Respondent's education		
None	26	39	36	56
1–3	43	45	48	32
4 or more	31	16	16	12
TOTAL	100	100	100	100

SOURCE: Fowler, 1965.

cash loans, found that, while higher-income respondents with lower education did not report their loans better than low-income respondents, those with more education did (Table 4). The authors suggest that the latter group may be more understanding of social research and thus report more conscientiously. However, not all motives of the higher educated lead to reporting accuracy. Several studies show that, at times, motives act to inhibit valid responses. Lansing et al. (1961), for example, found that higher-educated respondents were somewhat more likely than the lower-educated to over-report the size of their savings account by $1,000 or more. Weiss (1968) also found that while higher-educated respondents are generally more accurate, they are poorer reporters of some information, as shown by the following: More higher- than lower-educated respondents reported they voted though official records showed they did not (Table 5). When asked whether children had failed to successfully complete a grade in school, higher-educated respondents were less likely to report failures that school records showed had occurred. Thus, conformity to perceived norms, or factors of self esteem, may result in poor reporting. Where such values, attitudes, or perception of the desired response varies by educational groups, we may expect differential bias in the results.

TABLE 4
*Report of
savings
accounts by
educational
level* (in
percent)*

Reporting of savings accounts (compared to records)	8 grades or less	High school	College
	Education of respondent		
Underreported by $1,000 or more	29	32	31
Overreported by $1,000 or more	9	3	16
Accurate within $1,000	62	65	53

* For those respondents within each educational group reporting a savings balance.
SOURCE: Lansing, Ginsburg, & Braaten, 1961.

	Education of respondent		
	8 grades or less	Grades 9 thru 11	Grade 12 or higher
Nonvoters reporting voting	23	21	28
Voters reporting nonvoting	10	3	6
Respondents not reporting child who failed	50	46	58

SOURCE: Weiss, 1968.

TABLE 5
Reported voting behavior by educational level (in percent)

In looking at the characteristics of college students and graduates in this volume, some restrictions are imposed and some problems are encountered. Very little systematic survey data exists before 1940, so that the correlates of higher education explored are dated within the last three decades, most of them from the last one or two. One difficulty in utilizing findings from previously conducted surveys is that the methodology of one organization or of one survey is not duplicated by another. Questions used on one study are frequently not repeated on others, so that it is often difficult to establish trends. Also, data may not exist for certain periods. Changes reflected in data may be questionable because of variations in question wording, sampling techniques, or even in coding and analysis procedures.

Most of the studies reported are national in scope. Most of them used large numbers of individuals, so that there is seldom need for concern over small samples. Studies of individual schools, of a college's alumni, or of the population of a single city may, on occasion, be insightful, but they are not necessarily regarded as representative of higher education as a social institution and, although interesting, are potentially misleading. These studies, therefore, are not generally reported.

One area in which this exclusion is not well maintained is in studies of what happens during the college experience—developing correlates in the transition from freshman to senior. Most of the older studies in this area are of single institutions or of a small group of them, and generalizations of the results depend on the occasional instances of replication.

Since almost any social survey includes some measure of educational attainment, the data sources are vast. No attempt is made to cover all studies. Rather the focus is on sampling the available studies and reporting as diverse a set of correlates as can be found without including all studies that may support a particular association of some factor with education. Many of the findings reported here have been replicated, although a few are unique to one particular study.

Some judgment has also been exercised in selecting topics that hold some broad interest, and in summarizing the major results that typify findings in those areas without detailing all results or accounting for topics that were judged of very narrow interest. Examples of what is regarded as holding limited interest are the following: College graduates own more automobiles and drive farther. Starch (1969) finds that they are half again as likely, compared with high school graduates or those with some college, to own equipment such as a clothes dryer or dishwasher; to drink wine; to invest in bonds, stocks, or shares of mutual funds, or to travel by air. Holders of postgraduate degrees are particularly likely to own typewriters, to have had passports for foreign travel, and to own musical instruments. Educational attainment also appears to be positively correlated with level of serum uric acid, which is associated with achievement drives (Dunn, Brooks, Mausner, Rodnan, & Cobb, 1963).

We excluded studies that mask findings on educational attainment by merging that single measure with others it is usually highly related to, such as complex indexes of socioeconomic status (SES). Most of the literature on child rearing, for instance, is presented by SES rather than by education as a single factor. Status crystallization is not so widespread that any one of the major components of SES can stand for the others, and interesting divergencies from modal patterns are reported for cases in which components of SES are not matched. Thus this volume deals with only those studies that have kept education as a clear and separate variable.

In an interpretation of findings, however, this network of related variables presents a mixture of problems. Educational attainment correlates moderately with many variables. For instance, achieving a college degree is related to a good life, subsequent earnings, occupational status, and participation in society, and to similar antecedent characteristics in one's parents. What is the pattern of causation? Few studies have made any effort to dissect the contributions of these and other factors, and one is left with no explanation of the interdependence of a whole set of variables. The complex interactions are probably more important than the individual sets of relationship.

For instance, quartile groupings of ability or of socioeconomic status are each discriminating predictors of college attendance. But youth, men or women, in the upper quartile of ability *and* socio-economic status have a probability of about .85 of going to college. Drop to the next quartile of ability for men, and the probability is .65, and at the next quartile .36 — all still in the top quarter of SES. Ability makes a difference. Within the top quarter of ability for men, a drop to the next two quarters of SES is less pronounced, giving probabilities of attendance of .73 and .70; but the bottom quartile of SES, *still in the top ability group,* yields a likelihood of only .48 (.34 for women). SES makes a difference. There is no doubt that combinations of variables of this sort are powerful predictors and are more insightful explainers of college opportunity and success than when they are alone (Flanagan & Cooley, 1966). High ability is more important in getting into college than high SES, but the latter certainly helps.

Similarly, almost all college graduates achieve middle-class status — in income and occupation. Among those who attend college but drop out, the probability is about .66, so that SES in its upper groupings is highly associated with college achievement. One must recognize that the correlates of educational achievement often develop through intermediary factors such as occupational status and income resources, and should be regarded as secondary- or tertiary-level consequences of educational attainment.

Differences in the general adult population that relate to differences in educational attainment can be conceptualized as consequences arising out of three factors: admissions selection, being in college, and having a college education. Some of the correlates of education at the college level arise out of the conditions of admission, or self-selection in entry. Type of secondary school, academic performance, interest in academic work, ability to pay and to delay the role of income earner, and parental influence — all contribute to getting into college. But they also contribute to characteristics of the college graduate. The student who is brighter than half of his peers when he enters college will be in the same position when he gets out. The academic achiever may do well after graduation in the occupations that require continuing academic skills. The parental support that encourages educational success also has some influence on other phases of achievement. So many of the factors associated with a background of college or university degrees may reflect circumstances that led to the college experience more than they reflect characteristics acquired during higher education.

Other correlates of education at the college level arise out of the college experience itself. It is obvious that many things happen. Most students are exposed to new knowledge. Many get prepared to start a job as a teacher, doctor, lawyer, social worker, engineer, or other professional. Vocational preparation and general knowledge in the liberal-arts tradition are clear functions of a college. If college does not always provide specific skill training, it often serves as a base and a symbol of ability, ambition, and persistence that opens doors to business positions and other opportunities. But it is not so clear what else is learned in college: How do values change? Are there consequences of the engrossing and intensive exposure to a youth culture "away from home"? What are the correlates of a continued moratorium on adult commitments or a premature set of commitments in a somewhat socially disconnected situation? How do students change in the four or more years of higher education?

Trow (1967) and Feldman (1969) have described some of the methodological problems and research issues associated with investigating the impact of the college experience. The study, typically, is in terms of average differences between seniors and freshmen. These comparisons must be interpreted cautiously.

Class comparisons sometimes assume that what is being asked in questionnaries, interviews, and scales stays the same in meaning over four years of life. "Liking study," for instance, may refer to very different material and different behavior, with different payoffs, between beginning and later years. Changes in characteristics may be a pattern of selective withdrawal or late transfers, so that while few individuals change, the composition and distribution of the class changes. Class comparisons assume that a given freshman class is similar to that of four years before or four years hence. A university may also change in whom it admits, attracts, or allows to stay. Class comparisons also usually assume that the measured factors have remained steady in the population, indicating that changes are due to the college experience and not to shifts in the larger society.

One wonders about differentiating the impact of the college experience from the impact of societal events and from the changing characteristics of the total college scene as experienced by a student—when comparing reports, studies, and accounts of the college student body of the late sixties with Jacob's (1957) findings on students of the early fifties. He offers a composite picture that he says applied to at least three-quarters of them. The college student of the 1950s, Jacob writes, was "gloriously contented, unabashedly self-centered, dutifully responsive toward government," and loyal to his alma mater. This student also showed tolerance for diversity, a willingness to accept (but not initiate) change in society's mores and folkways, an acceptance of traditional moral and religious values, and little interest in international affairs (Jacob, 1957).

Other correlates of a college degree arise out of the kind of lives led by people who have them. Opportunities change, and access to new experiences, roles, and statuses improve, including the opportunity to go on to even more specialized education. Some characteristics link with the college experience, and some develop out of the new milieu in which the graduate begins to live. College graduates travel more (particularly in foreign countries) than those with less education. This is due partly to opportunities created by their jobs and occupations, partly to their broader interests, but also to their ability to pay for such trips. Many of these trips come long after the college experience. But interest in going may trace back directly to college studies and student associates. Deutsch (1969) in a study at three universities showed that college serves to internationalize and cosmopolitanize a student's perspectives and values. Students expect to travel abroad. They support international exchanges. Their lives and interests have a more international flavor and focus. There is a life-long sequence of consequences of a college education in opportunities, events, and accomplishments. This continues as a person moves through adult life, raising children, creating interests, and providing opportunities that lead his children to choose college in turn.

2. Who Goes to College

Jo Anne Coble

The impact of higher education is, in one way, limited to those exposed to it. Limitations are set by the persons who try to get into college and by admissions personnel who accept applications. Pressures that have led to explosive growth of applicants have reduced the national influence of admissions gatekeepers, except as they continue to screen students for particular institutions. But some have altered or relaxed old criteria, and new institutions have sprung up to meet the needs of aspiring students who otherwise would not be served. Thus, the number and variety of people going to college have risen spectacularly.

This increase has been so phenomenal that we are near the point at which young people who do *not* go to college will be in the minority. There are undoubtedly characteristics of "being a minority" that affect self-evaluations and the way that society looks at the minority group. But "becoming a majority" also means that the sense of elitism or privilege is largely diluted. Consequently the simple aspect of the proportion of the population that becomes exposed to the college experience does have some social impact.

Studies over the past generation on educational attainment and aspiration lead inescapably to the conclusions that the student's interests, intelligence (measured by standardized tests), father's education, financial resources, and sex are independently related to getting into college (Brim, Glass, Neulinger, & Firestone, 1969; Folger, Astin, & Bayer, 1969; Lavin, 1965; Sewell, 1964; Sewell & Armer, 1966; Sewell, Haller, & Straus, 1957; Sewell & Shah, 1967, 1968a&b). This chapter does not delve into these well-known factors, but rather looks at some of the dynamics of how they operate in the family unit, among peers, and in the school.

STRUCTURAL
PROPERTIES
OF THE
FAMILY UNIT

Given ability and interest, what happens to a child in a family with limited financial resources? What are his chances of going to college in relation solely to the family structure? To answer that, one must know the number of siblings in the family, the ratio of girls to boys, the ordinal position of each sibling, the years separating each child, and the occupational status of the father.

According to most authors, students from large families are substantially less likely to attend college than those from smaller families. The assumption is that the larger the family, the more difficult it is for a given child to be allocated sufficient funds. Some would add that it depends on the ordinal position of the child in the family; if he is first born or last born he probably has a better chance than any other siblings in the family. Others note that it depends on the child's sex — a male child having an advantage over his female siblings.

There is no simple answer, and none of the factors mentioned can be considered in isolation of other conditions present in the family structure. The work of Adams and Meidam (1968) represents one of the more complete accounts of the effects of the family structure on college attendance. Adams and Meidam raised the question of the number of siblings it takes to introduce an effect on the educational opportunities of a given offspring. According to their findings, the limiting effect of sibship size does not appear sharply restrictive until the female is one of four siblings, or the male is one of five in white-collar families. While children of blue-collar families start out with fewer chances of college attendance in comparison with white-collar families, significant effects from sibship size begin showing up for females with four or five siblings, and for males with seven or more siblings. The implication is that, beyond these sizes, each additional offspring makes it less likely that a given child will attend college. In the case of an only child, there is, of course, a greater educational advantage regardless of sex (Table 6).

Given these conditions, how does the sex ratio of the siblings further increase or decrease an offspring's chances of attending college? Drawing from the work of Adams and Meidam, we know that males have had an opportunity advantage over females in our educational and occupational systems. In terms of a limited resource concept, no sex-ratio difference is now present for white-collar females. As the number of brothers increases in blue-collar families, however, college attendance of their sisters decreases

	Sex, father's occupational status, and sibship size	Percent with some college
TABLE 6	White-collar males	
College attendance by	1	81
sibship size,	2	86
controlling for	3	78
sex and father's	4	89
occupational	5	62
status	6+	33
	Blue-collar males	
	1	47
	2	39
	3	29
	4	35
	5	29
	6	28
	7+	13
	White-collar females	
	1	86
	2	80
	3	82
	4	69
	5	57
	6+	42
	Blue-collar females	
	1	40
	2	30
	3	30
	4	33
	5	17
	6	20
	7+	16

SOURCE: Adams & Meidam, 1968.

precipitously. This suggests that males in blue-collar families have first claim on family resources allotted for education. It should be understood, however, that, to date, researchers have not widely investigated cultural differences as they relate to family structure and educational attainment. For instance, the black female has historically been given more of an opportunity to advance educationally and occupationally than has the black male. Particularly in black families of low socioeconomic status, the emphasis has been on educating the black female at any given level of formal training. The bulk of available research hypotheses and conclusions does not reflect this, but rather the habits and culture of "majority" Americans, or where group differences are masked, of Americans in general.

Another structural factor is the concept of child spacing, the number of years separating siblings. Adams and Meidam (1968) postulate that, within each sex and status category, the individual whose sibling is separated from him by five or more years is more likely to attend college. In fact, as the number of years increases, the chance of either or both attending college also increases. Presumably closely spaced siblings face greater competition for limited monetary support. Table 7 shows the likelihood of college attendance for individuals from two-child families, by space between siblings.

One of the unsettled issues among authors researching the family unit is whether there is a consistent pattern of birth-order differences in college attendance. Barger and Hall (1966), for example, found that when family size was controlled by research selection, no significant relationship appeared between birth order and educational attainment. Schacter (1963) says that earlier-born offspring have an educational advantage over later-born siblings. Bayer (1966) reported that the oldest and youngest siblings are about equal in likelihood of attending college when sex and socio-

TABLE 7
College attendance of individuals from two-child families, by age-space between siblings, controlling for sex and father's occupational status

Sex and father's occupational status	Years different in age	Percentage with some college
White-collar males	5+	97
	4—	83
White-collar females	5+	86
	4—	76
Blue-collar males	5+	44
	4—	35
Blue-collar females	5+	33
	4—	30

SOURCE: Adams & Meidam, 1968.

economic status are controlled by research selection, with middle children having the least chance. Single children, however, have the greatest educational advantage, according to Bayer. Adams and Meidam (1968), controlling for socioeconomic status, sex, and sibship size, found no consistent pattern resulting from birth order.

Obviously no single guiding hypothesis can be made. Authors use different control variables and methods of analysis and arrive at different conclusions regarding the same issue. In addition, birth-order effects, like sex-ratio trends, tend to be more heavily influenced by cultural traditions, habits, and values, rather than solely by economic considerations as in the case of sibship size and child spacing. As Elder (1962, Ch. 3) has noted, in the middle-class family the oldest child, especially a male, tends to bear a major portion of the parents' aspirations for their offspring. In the working-class family, however, the older children frequently have had to drop out even before completing high school in order to help the family economically. Ordinal position thus varies in its relation to education in families of higher and lower socioeconomic status.

SOCIAL-PSY-CHOLOGICAL PROPERTIES OF THE FAMILY UNIT The social-psychological properties of the family unit that stifle or enhance the likelihood of children attending college are not so well defined as the structural variables just described. Much of this section deals with some of the social-psychological dynamics arising from the family's social class position and the parents' values and aspirations, which operate to influence the child's expectations and ambitions regarding higher levels of education.

The family's socioeconomic status (SES), a mixture of several characteristics, is a factor that seems to influence all others in the question of who goes to college, first from an economic perspective and, secondly, in terms of the family's values, expectations, ambitions, and aspirations for its offspring. The two most important factors determining SES are the parents' education and occupation. From an economic perspective, college attendance is more likely for the offspring of white-collar parents. Although not all white-collar families are high SES, they fall, on the average, relatively higher in SES than blue-collar families, who are usually in the low SES category.

Parental education plays a different kind of role than occupation in the way it contributes to a variance in college attendance. Sewell and Shah (1968*b*) report that, in each category of SES and intelligence, the proportion of males and females planning to attend college is greater among those who perceived parental encouragement than among those who did not (see Table 8). Furthermore, both fathers' and mothers' educational achievements are positively and significantly related to parental encouragement, college plans, college attendance, and graduation from college (Sewell & Shah, 1968*a*). In effect these studies show how SES, defined in terms of parental education and occupation, can operate to influence variance in college attendance. The higher the parents' level on one or both of the items, the higher the SES and the greater a given offspring's chances of attending college.

Parental encouragement at any SES level tends to heighten the likelihood of a given offspring attending college. There seems to be no doubt that the nuclear family is the primary impetus for mobility, but there is some question as to which parent serves as the major catalyst. Ellis and Lane (1963) advanced the notion that it is the mother more often than the father whose reactions to the family's status in life is the stimulus for mobility. Sewell and Shah (1968*a*), however, contend that in cases of discrepant levels of educational achievement between parents, it is generally the father's education that exerts more influence on aspiration and achievement. But for children of low intelligence, it is the mother's education that exerts more influence.

In general, parental encouragement has its strongest effects on the college plans of males and females who score high on IQ and come from families of relatively high SES (Sewell & Shah, 1968*b*). Furthermore, the higher the level of SES the higher the level of educational aspirations even after sex, intelligence, and parental encouragement are controlled. In effect, SES contributes to the level of educational aspirations in complex ways that involve interaction between, and reinforcement of, many pressures. Obviously, many students from high SES grow up in a family atmosphere where the benefits of educational attainments are evident and where the accessibility of such opportunities is realized very early in a student's development. Krauss (1964) has pointed out that, in lower SES families, the support for educational aspiration often comes from older siblings who have had college experience and can serve as an example or a catalyst in stimulating the younger siblings and interesting them in pursuing a college education. There

TABLE 8
Percentages of students who planned to attend college, by socioeconomic status, measured intelligence, and perceived parental encouragement, separately for males and females

| | Males | | | Females | | |
| | Perceived parental encouragement: | | | Perceived parental encouragement: | | |
Socioeconomic status	Low	High	Total	Low	High	Total
	Low intelligence					
Low	1.1	16.8		1.1	17.0	
Lower middle	0.8	24.3		3.7	32.2	
Upper middle	4.6	34.1		4.1	33.3	
High	7.6	40.6		10.7	38.3	
TOTAL	2.2	29.8		3.0	31.8	
	Lower middle intelligence					
Low	4.2	31.4		1.6	23.0	
Lower middle	3.4	40.3		7.5	34.8	
Upper middle	4.8	40.2		6.3	45.4	
High	9.6	57.8		6.6	59.1	
TOTAL	4.4	44.5		4.9	45.0	
	Upper middle intelligence					
Low	8.7	41.3		3.6	36.4	
Lower middle	9.4	50.2		6.8	42.2	
Upper middle	15.6	59.6		6.4	47.6	
High	18.0	77.5		21.6	74.0	
TOTAL	11.8	61.8		7.0	57.2	
	High intelligence					
Low	13.0	53.2		11.9	53.8	
Lower middle	17.7	66.8		11.7	59.0	
Upper middle	12.5	73.0		19.8	64.8	
High	32.0	88.4		21.0	78.6	
TOTAL	16.6	77.3		15.2	70.7	
	Total					
Low	4.4	36.3	14.6	2.8	32.1	7.7
Lower middle	5.7	47.9	26.3	6.6	42.5	19.8
Upper middle	8.1	55.5	38.8	7.8	50.4	29.4
High	14.5	75.0	66.4	14.6	70.2	59.4
TOTAL	6.5	58.6	36.9	6.2	55.6	28.9
N	(2085)	(2906)	(4991)	(2880)	(2447)	(5327)

SOURCE: Sewell & Shah, 1968*b*.

are a number of "models" for students outside the family, some of which are discussed in the next section.

Spady (1967), in a study on educational mobility and access, asserts that the *relative* chances of boys from the lower social strata reaching and completing college, compared with the sons of college-educated fathers, have not kept pace with each other over time. Moreover, the relative probabilities of going to college, given graduation from high school, *and* graduating have dropped slightly for low-status sons (Table 9). While an increasing number of low-status sons have enrolled in institutions of higher education, Spady finds that there has been an even greater increase in enrollment and graduation of sons with college-educated fathers.

TABLE 9
Percentage of sons obtaining a given level of education, by age and father's education

Son's age	Father's education				Attainment gap (%) (col. 4− col. 1)
	Less than eight (1)	Some high school (2)	High school graduate (3)	Some college or more (4)	
	Reaching high school				
25–34	82.9	94.6	97.4	99.6	+16.7
35–44	78.7	92.7	97.7	98.8	+20.1
45–54	70.1	90.9	96.4	97.6	+27.5
55–64	60.4	85.8	88.4	93.0	+32.6
	Graduating from high school				
25–34	44.6	69.4	84.2	92.8	+48.2
35–44	41.2	59.5	79.6	92.8	+51.6
45–54	32.1	46.9	76.0	78.4	+46.3
55–64	19.6	34.3	58.9	73.9	+54.3
	Obtaining at least one year of college				
25–34	14.2	27.8	44.1	78.0	+63.8
35–44	14.4	22.0	44.9	70.4	+56.0
45–54	11.0	19.1	33.2	62.3	+51.3
55–64	8.4	15.0	31.4	47.3	+39.8
	Graduating from college				
25–34	6.5	16.6	24.9	51.7	+45.2
35–44	5.8	11.0	27.5	53.1	+46.3
45–54	5.4	8.9	14.5	37.7	+32.3
55–64	5.4	8.5	16.9	27.6	+22.2

SOURCE: Spady, 1967.

One of the most effective influences on educational aspirations outside the family is the school environment—particularly the high school. This is not to say that the elementary and junior high school experience does not play a part in influencing a student's evaluation of his own capabilities and potential; they play an extremely important role in the development of a child's self-concept, self-esteem, and academic ability. The high school experience, however, is crucial to a sense of competence, since it is the time of decision and the staging area for postsecondary activities. This can be the final phase of formal education for the student, or it can be a stepping-stone to further attainment. At this point, decisions must be made regarding his career objectives.

Looking at the broad picture, who is most likely to go to college and who is not? And, most importantly, what role does the high school environment play in shaping the decisions of these students? Through a tracking system, many high school students are restricted in their exposure to college preparation. If one assumes that this system efficiently weeds out those not capable of college work, then one need have no qualms about it. But if one lacks confidence in this early decision, then the question may arise about premature restriction to college opportunity.

The high school climate has an influence in shaping its students' abilities in so-called underachieving and overachieving schools. Michael (1961) reports that in the overachieving schools, ability accounts for the greatest proportion of variance in college attendance, while in underachieving schools, social class is more predictive of a student's educational future (Table 10). If a student attends an overachieving school, the aspirations and expectations of his peer group can influence his own educational plans. If the high school climate does not encourage college attendance, then social status appears to be a more important source of variation in college plans.

Undoubtedly teachers, counselors, and other significant individuals outside the family may be key sources of influence on any future plans a student makes concerning his educational and occupational goals. These individuals can serve as stimulators or dampeners of students' educational interests and aspirations. In a small sample study, Ellis and Lane (1963) found that nonfamilial influences on educational aspirations were greatest for students of lower social backgrounds. The chief source of outside support

TABLE 10
Percent of
seniors scoring
in the top
quarter of the
scholastic
aptitude test
who plan to
attend college,
according to
socioeducational
status of the
family and high
school climate

	High school climate†					All climates
Family status quintile*	V (hi)	IV	III	II	I (lo)	
5 (hi)	86	81	82	77	80	83
4	74	67	68	54	72	68
3	63	57	53	48	48	56
2	57	46	49	40	38	47
1 (lo)	57	48	46	45	44	47
All quintiles	77	65	62	51	50	65

* Family status quintiles represent the distribution of characteristics within the community, including education, occupation, financial resources, and cultural facilities.
† High school climate is related to both high school and community attributes. The proportion of the senior class in the top two family-status quintiles was used as the criterion: I—Schools with less than 20 percent of the senior class in the top two family-status quintiles; II—Schools with 20–29 percent of the seniors from such homes; III—Schools with 30–39 percent of the seniors from such homes; IV—Schools with 40–49 percent of the seniors from such homes; V—Schools with a majority of their senior class coming from privileged homes.
SOURCE: Michael, 1961.

was a high school teacher. They suggest that the teacher's significance in the mobility process stemmed from the lower-class parents' inability to give effective direction to the aspirations stimulated in the child. The number of nonfamilial influences reported in the study reaches its maximum among lower-class girls. The lower-class students were talented youth who excelled in criteria used to measure academic potential, so that it is not surprising that their high school teachers exhibited an active interest in their educational endeavors.

The student is not a passive participant in the development of

TABLE 11   *Number of students' acquaintances planning to attend college and students' post-high school plans (in percent)*

Student's post-high school plans	Working-class students				Middle-class students			
	None	Some	Most	All	None	Some	Most	All
College	10	29	60	81	(3)	47	77	83
Technical school	45	35	23	14	(5)	27	12	17
No further education	45	36	18	6	(8)	25	10	0
TOTAL	100	100	101	101	(16)	99	99	100
N	(43)	(177)	(129)	(36)	(16)	(91)	(112)	(47)

SOURCE: Krauss, 1964.

TABLE 12   *Degree of participation in extracurricular activities and students' post-high school plans (in percent)*

Student's post-high school plans	Working-class students			Middle-class students		
	Not very active	*Fairly active*	*Extremely active*	*Not very active*	*Fairly active*	*Extremely active*
College	28	50	74	55	66	80
Technical school	36	29	14	22	21	13
No further education	37	22	12	24	13	7
TOTAL	101	101	100	101	100	100
N	(199)	(138)	(50)	(101)	(120)	(46)

SOURCE: Krauss, 1964.

his educational plans. Certain clues arising from his activities, interests, choice of friends, and status in the school indicate the direction he will take, in terms of his educational objectives.

Krauss (1964) points out that college-oriented working-class students tend to have friends and acquaintances who also have college aspirations and tend to be extremely active in extracurricular activities. Moreover, these students are more likely to attend a predominantly middle-class school. The trend that Krauss points out, however, is not confined to the activities of working-class youth. Tables 11 and 12 indicate the same pattern of extracurricular activity and choice of acquaintances for college-oriented middle-class youth. Krauss suggests a number of possible dynamics operating in the family and school environment that may explain how college-oriented working-class students come to have middle-class values. The major implication is, however, that the social contact and interaction of working-class and middle-class students probably encourages the working-class students to take the middle-class students as their reference group and thus accept the values and ideals of that group.

3. The Impact of the College Experience

Gerald Gurin

The following chapters will present some ways in which the values, orientations, and lives of college-educated people differ from those of people who never went to college. We have already suggested that such findings do not offer conclusive evidence that the college experience was a critical factor in the development of these differences. A limitation on such an interpretation is the factor of *selection.* Differences in these characteristics may reflect the different background characteristics that distinguish people who go to college from those who do not.

Since the college experience is not randomly assigned to individuals, one can never be sure of the relative influence of selective factors and college experience on postcollege values and behavior. But some answers to this question lie in the vast research literature that refers to students during their college years and focuses on the changes that they undergo. Is there evidence that college students change between their freshman and senior years in ways that are consistent with the differences between college and noncollege people observed in national cross-sectional studies? What evidence is there that these changes persist in later life? There is at least inferential evidence that a given difference between college and noncollege populations does reflect some impact of the college experience where research studies show that characteristics change between the freshman and senior years, that changes are greater for college students than for comparable people who did not go to college, and that these changes persist into the postcollege years.

We should note that the logic of this argument does not apply to all college and noncollege differences in orientation and behavior reviewed in this volume. It is not relevant to those characteristics that arise out of postcollege status, life opportunities, and economic resources that are made available by a college degree, rather than during the college experience itself. Nor is it relevant in those instances where the college experience has a long-range impact that is not evident in the college years. One should, therefore, approach this chapter's review of the college impact literature with this caution in mind: While the demonstration of change in college helps support the interpretation that a given orientation among the college educated reflects the impact of the college experience, the lack of demonstrable change in college cannot be taken as conclusive proof that the experience had no impact.

Moreover, even when research studies seem to indicate the impact of college, the mere demonstration of freshman-to-senior change does not indicate the meaning of the change, the reasons that college had a critical impact in this area, or those aspects of the college experience that were particularly crucial and relevant. The impact may reflect the influence of academic aspects of the college experience. It may reflect the nature of the social environment exposed to in college. It may reflect less about the college experience per se than it does the opportunity college provides for a four-year moratorium for thinking through issues of identity and values. The college-student studies do not provide definitive answers to these questions. For some suggestive evidence, we look at the more analytic studies of college impact that have attempted to relate change in college to different characteristics of the college and to specific aspects of the college experience.

One final question will concern us in this chapter. The research literature by its nature relates to college impact in the past, particularly the past 20 years. In our introductory chapter, we have noted the great changes colleges are undergoing, as we move toward an era of higher education for a majority of our population. Can the findings of these studies be projected to estimate the impact of college in the years ahead? Two questions are relevant. First, is there evidence that institutions (like community and commuter colleges) particularly addressed to the needs of students of lower academic preparation, lower socioeconomic status, and more vocational interests, have different impact than the traditional institutions of higher education? Secondly, is there evidence that these students are affected differently in their values and orientations, regardless of the college they go to?

To summarize, this chapter approaches the literature on college impact with three sets of questions:

1 What is the evidence on college impact? In what ways do students change in college? Are the changes greater than for people who do not go to college? Do the changes persist into the postcollege years?

2 What are the relationships between change in college and different characteristics and aspects of the college experience?

3 Does college have different impacts on students differing in academic preparation, socioeconomic status, and college goals?

EVIDENCE OF COLLEGE IMPACT The increasing interest in the impact of higher education, as well as the bewildering mass of empirical studies bearing on the issue, have stimulated several attempts over the past decade to integrate and make some sense of the relevant research literature. The beginning of this effort was Jacob's *Changing Values in College* (1957), its culmination in Feldman and Newcomb's comprehensive and definitive study, *The Impact of College on Students* (1969). The latter work has been particularly valuable in pulling together the vast literature and pointing up critical issues, and we have drawn on it heavily in this chapter.

The first question we have posed, whether the research studies show that certain values, attitudes, and orientations of students tend to change in consistent ways between the freshman and senior years, is admittedly oversimplified. It is phrased in terms of average change between the freshman and senior year, ignoring that any average represents the balancing of contradictory individual changes. It also ignores the sophisticated issue of differential change in different types of colleges, or under varying experiences at a given college. But the gross phrasing does address the issue of whether—regardless of individual, institutional, and intra-institutional variations—there may be some common elements in the college experience that tend to produce an impact in a given direction.

Given the crudity of the measure, it is significant that certain consistencies do appear. As summarized in Feldman and Newcomb (1969, **1**, Ch. 2, & **2**, Tables 2A, 2D, 2E, 2H), most studies show that students going through college increase their interest in aesthetic and cultural values, decrease their adherence to traditional religion and other traditional values, become more relativistic and less moralistic in their ethical judgments. They also take an increasingly liberal rather than conservative position on political and socioeconomic issues and become more open-minded as measured by scales on authoritarianism, dogmatism, ethnocentrism, and prejudice. The findings in these areas tend to be consistent in many studies and in different types of colleges. They are documented not only in cross-sectional studies that compare freshmen and seniors at a given point in time, but also in longitudinal studies that have followed the same students through their four-year college career.[1]

The findings on open-mindedness are particularly relevant. They are a critical aspect of the impact that one hopes a college education would have. They also are consistent with some of the major findings from national cross section surveys on the value differences between college and noncollege populations. These surveys have consistently shown that the college educated are more open and liberal in their attitudes toward civil rights, prejudice, and civil liberties. The findings in the college impact literature are particularly impressive in this area. As summarized in Feldman and Newcomb (1969, vol. II, table 2H), a large number of studies, longitudinal as well as cross-sectional, in many diverse types of colleges, all document the change toward more openness, less prejudice, and less tendency toward dogmatic and stereotypic thinking.

Selvin and Hagstrom in their study of Berkeley students found:

. . . that the very marked difference in libertarianism among students of different social origins originally found is even more marked among lower division (freshman and sophomore) students, but has largely disappeared among upper division (junior and senior) students. This finding has a number of implications. It strengthens the possibility that increases in libertarianism between freshman and senior year are the product of actual changes in attitudes, rather than the result of disproportionate dropouts

---

[1] Cross-sectional studies are limited because they assume that if freshmen and seniors differ at a given point in time, similar differences would have been obtained if seniors had been compared with what they were as freshmen four years previously. This ignores such factors as differential dropout from college and historical changes that might affect the characteristics and orientations of the freshman class over a four-year period. Most studies of college impact have this design. However, longitudinal studies are being done increasingly, and, as Feldman and Newcomb (1969) document, their findings tend to be consistent with those of the cross-sectional studies.

among the least libertarian, since the increases are the greatest among those groups originally lowest in libertarianism. But more important, the finding sheds light on one of the most important functions of higher education—its tendency to reduce the influence of prior social statuses and experiences, and forge a new set of shared identities and attitudes among college graduates (Trow, 1967).

While the studies reported and summarized in the research literature agree on the direction of these changes, there has been a great deal of disagreement over their meaning and interpretation. Specifically, some commentators have questioned whether these changes represent a true liberalization, a significant movement in the direction of increasing tolerance and flexibility. Jacob (1957) is particularly identified with this skeptical view. His conclusion, in the landmark review of the literature on college impact, was that college had minimal effect on a student's values. He noted many of the same kinds of changes from freshman to senior year, including the changes in tolerance and prejudice that we have quoted (Jacob, 1957, p. 48). What Jacob minimized was not the change itself, but the meaning of the change. Noting that our country as a whole had become increasingly committed to tolerance over the preceding generation, Jacob interpreted the changes in college as reflecting an adaptation to a college norm reflecting the larger societal norm, rather than the development of an internalized commitment in this area. He wrote that, as the country changed:

. . . college students quickly discovered, if they had not before, that prejudice was now considered unbecoming to an "enlightened" American citizen. College thus became an effective medium of communication for a newly prescribed social value. . . .

To call this process a *liberalization* of student values is a misnomer. The impact of the college experience is rather to *socialize* the individual, to refine, polish, and "shape up" his values so that he can fit comfortably into the ranks of American college alumni (Jacob, 1957).

Jacob's skepticism was undoubtedly affected by the fact that he was writing during the "apathetic fifties," as well as by a philosophic and ethical orientation that questioned the meaning of values that were not being implemented in some meaningful action and commitment. To some extent his criticism reflected a specific interpretation of the relationship between values and action. Values can be significant even if not activated at a particular time; the values that Jacob questioned in the fifties undoubtedly provided the underpinning for the activism and commitment on the campuses of the sixties.

However, the kind of criticism that Jacob offered has been raised by others as well. Particularly interesting are the conclusions that Katz and his associates reached in their longitudinal study of students at Berkeley and Stanford (Katz, 1968). As a long-time associate of Nevitt Sanford, Katz is part of the tradition that has conceptualized open-mindedness and tolerance as aspects of the very general personality syndrome of nonauthoritarianism. Designating this dimension as a personality characteristic is indicative of their belief in its centrality and depth. This tradition also has viewed college as an environment with unusual potential for inducing change. In spite of this orientation, Katz concluded his study with the feeling that deep change was less prevalent than he had anticipated, that "we had a greater expectation of profound alterations of character among our interviewees than was warranted" (Katz, 1968, p. 7).

With specific reference to change in the nonauthoritarian syndrome, an analysis by Korn (Katz, 1968, chap. 3) is particularly relevant. Korn analyzed freshman-to-senior change on several personality scales relating to the syndrome. By conducting his analysis at an item-by-item level, Korn arrived at a conclusion very similar to Jacob's. By separating those items on which much change occurred from those showing little freshman-to-senior change, he concluded that change seemed more a process of socialization than of personality restructuring.

Other investigators have made much the same point, although phrasing it in terms of "sophistication" rather than "socialization." They have cautioned that it is important to separate the extent to which the tests of liberalism and tolerance and openness are measuring a genuine increase in flexibility and tolerance, rather than the fact that students, as they pass through college, acquire a sophistication that cautions them against accepting very crude and obvious stereotypes. As will be noted in the discussion of Stember's work on prejudice (1961) in Chapter 5, college students change much more on items that represent very blatant and obvious stereotypes than they do on some of the subtler manifestations of prejudice. This does not mean that increased sophistication is all that the freshman-to-senior change represents (cf. Brown and

Datta, 1959), but it is clear that the changes that do occur are not so simple as the words *tolerance* and *open-mindedness* imply.

In the criticisms and questions that Jacob and others have raised, there is some tendency to minimize the significance of a value change because it is embedded in a broad social and cultural context. Jacob particularly suggests that this means that the changes are not "internalized" and deeply meaningful to the individuals manifesting the change. While we question the implication that this somehow makes a value change less meaningful, it is important to be reminded that studies documenting these freshman-to-senior changes toward increasing openness and tolerance have been made during a time when the culture as a whole was changing in these directions. This suggests that a college education in itself is not necessarily liberalizing, but it has served that function within the cultural context of the past 30 years. In making this point, Jacob quoted figures from Stouffer's study (1955) on attitudes toward civil liberties. This study indicated that among people aged 60 and over there were no differences between the attitudes of high school and college graduates, whereas in the group below 40 the college graduates were much more tolerant:

Thus as the whole pattern of American culture moved toward tolerance, during the last 25 years, the college experience made for even greater tolerance. The college student acquired—or perhaps anticipated—the outlook of his generation, only more so, but the fact of having had a college education did *not* make the *older* generation either more disposed toward a tolerant outlook per se, or more flexible than others of their age in changing their original mind set to accord with the trend of the times (Jacob, 1957, p. 48).

We will note a very similar pattern of findings in our discussion (Chapter 7) of the different relationship between education and civil rights attitudes for the older and younger generation. While such findings do not negate the significance of the change in recent college generations, they do suggest that education in itself is no automatic panacea for those who value its potential for increasing flexibility and tolerance. We will return to this issue of college as a socializing agent and facilitator of *prevailing* cultural tendencies in our concluding comments in this chapter.

We have focused on freshman-to-senior changes in tolerance and open-mindedness because they have been very dominant in the studies of college students and because this area is often viewed as a major outcome of a liberal education. But we will briefly note the findings on within-college change in some other areas where differences between colleges and noncollege populations are discussed in the following chapters.

Changes in Occupational Orientation In Chapter 4 we will note that college-educated people differ from those without a college education in their orientation toward the world of work. Many studies document the fact that they look for different things in a job. The college educated more often stress ego gratification and the nature of the work itself; the less educated more often stress extrinsic factors such as income, security, and working conditions. At first glance, these differences would seem to reflect the impact of college on the type of job one can obtain, a byproduct rather than the direct effect of the college experience on the student's values and orientations. Jobs available to those of higher education typically offer more possibilities for the gratification of needs for challenge and diversity.

There are, however, a number of studies of freshman-to-senior change in college that suggest that a college education may have a more direct impact in developing these differential orientations toward work. Feldman and Newcomb (1969, 2, Table 2C) summarize a number of studies in this area that show a consistent tendency for seniors to differ from freshmen in the relative importance they assign to intrinsic rather than extrinsic gratifications in a job. The differences occur mainly because seniors show less concern over the extrinsic aspects of a job. Particularly striking is the consistent finding that security becomes a much less important consideration. The findings on the development of intrinsic orientations are less clear. Seniors show somewhat more inclination to stress the importance of a job that challenges their ability and gives them an opportunity to be more creative, but the differences here are less impressive than the decreases in security and other extrinsic motivations.

In short, the findings seem to suggest that freshmen go to college with ideas that give considerable importance to both intrinsic and extrinsic aspects of a job, and that differentiation occurs by the diminishing significance of the extrinsic aspects. The studies are somewhat ambiguous in what they suggest about the impact of the college experience. The findings may reflect the security of seniors approaching the favorable job market of the past generation — when these studies were done—rather than any unusual impact of college in stimulating an individual to look inwardly, rather than externally, for gratification in the job and other areas of life.

Two other areas where college and noncollege differences are noted in later chapters have also been the object of college change studies: *political interest and involvement* and *positive adjustment and mental health.* In both of these areas, the within-college studies are not consistent with the relationships with education that have been documented in the national cross-section surveys.

Political Involvement and Interest

In contrast to the consistent findings on change in college in the *direction* of political attitudes, there is no clear indication that college students develop in the *extent* of their political interest and involvement. Summarizing several studies in this area, Feldman and Newcomb (1969, pp. 22–23) noted that the findings are ambiguous and inconsistent, and by no means point to greater political interest and involvement of seniors when contrasted with freshmen entering college. Unlike some of the other findings noted, therefore, the data on within-college changes in this area do not anticipate the survey findings that college graduates indicate greater political interest and participation than do people who never attended college. There are a number of other possible explanations for these findings.

The greater involvement of the college educated may come from their greater stake in the social system; it may reflect selective factors that bring people of higher political involvement to college in the first place; or it may reflect a long-range impact of college not discernible in the college years. At any rate, the evidence does not suggest any unusual development of this interest and involvement during the college years. This may seem surprising given the political turmoil on the campuses of the 1960s and the supposed radicalization that occurs on them. The full impact of these events is yet to be documented. Most studies of student activism, however, highlight the extent to which involvement in activism is affected by the background characteristics and value orientations that a student brings with him to the college scene (cf. Katz, 1968, Ch. 11; Flacks, 1967).

Psychological Adjustment and Well-being

Similar comments may be made on the findings from a number of studies comparing freshmen and seniors on different measures of psychological adjustment. As indicated in the discussion in

Chapter 5, data from postcollege studies suggest that well-educated people evidence more psychological adjustment, at least in terms of the concepts and measures used in the studies. No such consistent relationships appear in the numerous studies that have attempted to trace the changes in college students through different measures of psychological well-being (cf. Feldman and Newcomb, 1969, **2**, Table 2N).

As we noted in our introductory comments in this chapter, these negative findings on freshman-to-senior change do not mean that the college experience is irrelevant to the later increased political interest or psychological well-being of the more highly educated. The survey findings that the college educated are more politically involved and better psychologically adjusted may reflect the long-range impact of the college experience—not evident in the senior year—as well as the indirect effects that come from life-styles and resources that a college education makes available. But to the extent that changes in the college years help buttress the interpretation that college has an impact, we are less certain about the direct impact of the college experience on political involvement and psychological well-being.

HIGH SCHOOL GRADUATES NOT ATTENDING COLLEGE The demonstration that students change in college does not, of course, offer conclusive evidence that the college experience was the significant factor causing the change. At the simplest level, we would want to compare the changes of the college students with the changes of comparable high school seniors who did not go to college. Such a comparative study would also not be conclusive since one cannot equate college attenders and nonattenders on all relevant factors that affected the decision whether or not to go to college. The two groups by definition are not completely comparable. But a comparative study at least takes into consideration such obvious factors as socioeconomic background, academic ability, and initial position on the attitude and value scale by which change is being measured. A comparative study also avoids the obvious error of attributing to college a change that may be reflecting the general growth patterns of all postadolescents in our society.

With the vast accumulation of research on student change, it is surprising that only a handful of empirical studies compares changes in college students with those of high school seniors who did not attend college (cf. Plant, 1965; Trent & Medsker, 1968). But the findings are consistent in suggesting that, while high school graduates who do not attend college tend to change somewhat in the same direction as the college attenders, their changes are not as great. The studies also suggest that students who drop out before completing college change more than the nonattenders, but less than the college graduates. In a sense, impact seems to be related to the time spent in college (Plant, 1962, 1965; Trent and Medsker, 1968).

Trent and Medsker provide the most impressive evidence on the comparative changes of college and noncollege groups. The sample of high school seniors in their original testing in 1959 was large and representative (10,000 high school seniors in 37 high schools in 16 communities in Pennsylvania, California, and throughout the Midwest). They were able to test a large proportion of this sample four years later in 1963 and compare people who had spent the intervening years in college (for all or part of the four years) with several other groups who had not gone to college (particularly men and women who spent the four years working and women who were housewives). One major advantage of their large sample was that they were able to compare the changes of people differing in socioeconomic status and academic ability, so that they could test the extent to which greater change in college might be a function of the differential backgrounds and academic abilities of the college attenders and nonattenders. Among several scales on which they focused their analysis of four-year change, one was the social maturity scale of the Omnibus Personality Inventory, a scale that developed out of the Sanford tradition of studies of authoritarianism. The scale attempts to measure the nonauthoritarianism syndrome, the "open, flexible, critical, objective, non-judgmental" way of thinking that is one of the major areas on which the studies of college change have focused. Thus the Trent and Medsker study provides the best data available on the comparison of the college changed and noncollege changed in this critical dimension.

The findings of Trent and Medsker are quite striking. When we compare those who spent four years in college with those who were employed during the four years, we find that both groups increased on the social maturity scale, but the increase was much greater for the college group (the employed group averaged an increase of 3.5 standard points compared to an average of 10 standard points for the college group).[2] It is of particular significance that the same relative change was apparent even when socioeconomic status and academic ability were controlled; that is, the differences in the changes of the college attenders and nonattenders were just as great for the students from low socioeconomic backgrounds and with low Scholastic Aptitude Test (SAT) scores as for the students with higher socioeconomic background and SAT scores. Thus, the fact that college students showed greater changes away from authoritarianism cannot be attributed to the higher socioeconomic status and ability of people who go to college.

Findings from studies such as this still do not answer the question whether the decision to go to college reflects an openness that predisposes to change, so that the college attenders would have changed even if they had not gone. By its nature, such a question is not answerable in a society where college attendance is not determined by lottery. But these comparative studies do at least suggest that many of the changes observed among college students are not just the reflection of a general maturational or cultural process common to all young people of that age. While we do not yet have much data on comparative change in college and noncollege groups, available studies tend to support Jacob's view that the impact of college on liberalization and tolerance seems to represent, to some extent, a general cultural trend, but that among college students the trend is greatly intensified.

THE PERSIS- TENCE OF COLLEGE CHANGES
Given our interest in integrating the college impact studies with the national survey data on differences between the college and noncollege educated, the ideal study would follow students many years beyond college and relate their later attitudes and values to the changes they underwent during their college experience. To our knowledge there is only one study (Newcomb, Koenig, Flacks, & Warwick, 1967) with this design that focuses on the types of attitudes and values that are our concern in this chapter.

There have been some studies that have related change in college to the attitudes of graduates *a few years* after college. Such studies

---

[2] Parallel findings were obtained in a more modest study by Plant (1965). Plant followed up a number of students who had applied to San Jose State College, some of whom actually attended the college, others of whom did not attend. Four years later both groups had decreased on measures of dogmatism and authoritarianism, but the changes were greater among those who attended.

suggest that the attitudes and values that were held as seniors tend to persist in the immediate postcollege years (e.g., Freedman & Bereiter, 1963). Other studies have had more long-range follow-ups, looking at students a generation or so after their college years, but these have not necessarily been in areas of particular interest to this discussion (e.g., Strong, 1955, documents the persistence over a generation of vocational interests measured in the Strong Inventory). In addition, these long-range follow-ups have usually related attitudes *as seniors* to attitudes many years later, rather than relating later attitudes to the *changes* in college (e.g., Nelson 1956). While these studies generally show a good deal of consistency between senior attitudes and attitudes a generation later (although this consistency varies somewhat according to the nature of the value and attitude being studied), they are not conclusive since they do not relate these consistencies to within-college change. The consistency could be mainly among those people who changed minimally in college. Such studies do not answer the critical question of the persistence of the values of people who made significant changes in college.

There have also been studies that dealt inferentially with the issue of persistence by looking at different generations of alumni. Freedman's study (1967) of Vassar alumnae is an interesting example of this approach. In the 1950s, he conducted a study of the attitudes and values of six different decades of Vassar alumnae. One of the measures in his study was an early version of the non-authoritarianism scale. He found an interesting pattern of responses to this scale. The highest authoritarian scores were given by the alumnae from the class of 1904. The authoritarianism scores decreased in later classes reaching a low point in the classes of the 1930s and 1940s. Interestingly there was a significant *increase* in authoritarianism in the responses of the class of 1956. While there is no conclusive evidence that these differences represent the persistence of different attitudes and values acquired in college, they may be interesting reflections of the values and attitudes current at the time the women were in college. A decline in authoritarianism from the early 1900s to the 1940s seems to reflect the changing values in American society at large over these two generations. Similarly, the increase in authoritarianism of the class of 1956 seems to reflect the conservatism and American ethnocentrism of that period.

But, as we have indicated, such studies provide only inferential evidence on the persistence of change in college. One study bears directly on the persistence issue, though it deals only with women and with only one college. Newcomb (1943), in a classic study of the 1930s, documented the changes among many Bennington College girls from the conservative ideology of their backgrounds to the more liberal position on social and economic issues prevailing at the college. A generation later, in the 1960s, Newcomb and his associates (Newcomb et al., 1967) interviewed the same women to see what had happened to their attitudes and values. The findings indicated that those who became less conservative in college tended to persist in these orientations.

By comparing those whose changes persisted with those whose changes did not, Newcomb and his associates were also able to provide some information on the nature of the conditions that affect persistence. The major result was that persistence was related to finding—in the women's postcollege world—a social environment that supported their college change. Particularly significant were the values of the husbands. There was a very high correlation between persistence and marrying a man who also had nonconservative attitudes. The Bennington women were able to maintain their college changes over the years by choosing a social milieu that supported and reinforced their attitudes and values.

Since the research evidence on the relation of college change to persistence is meager, any conclusions must be tentative. Newcomb's Bennington findings suggest that college changes are likely to be persistent, and also some of the reasons for such persistence. Subsequent studies may prove these findings are typical.

For many people college may represent the last significant self-confronting experience. It provides an opportunity for meeting people of varying backgrounds with different ideas, at a time of life when self-examination is maximized and in an institution that legitimizes the identity task of exploring and reevaluating one's values and ideologies. This is true to some extent even though there is a great deal of selection in the choice of a college and experiences within it, and though many students do not maximize the opportunity for broadening their experiences. Even given self-selection, it is very likely that the chance and readiness to encounter different people and experiences is much greater in the college years than in the typical pattern a person follows in life after college, although college has been criticized as a conformity-inducing conservative influence. If this is so, one should expect to find the persistence of the college changes that Newcomb documented in his follow-up of the Bennington women.

COLLEGE
CHARACTER-
ISTICS RE-
LATED TO
STUDENT
CHANGE As research on college impact has developed in complexity and sophistication, researchers have turned from an interest in demonstrating widespread, freshman-to-senior change in a given area to relating these changes to particular characteristics of the college environment. An understanding of *why* college has an impact depends on the ability to delineate the types of college experiences critical for change in a given area.

Researchers have addressed this question at different levels. Studies have looked at the relationship of change to characteristics of the college as a whole, to subunits within the college (for example, major fields or residential arrangements), and to the immediate environment of the individual student (for example, his peer relationships). Moreover, within any given level the attempt to tie change to different characteristics of the environment has been approached with different degrees of complexity. Those who take the total college as the basic unit of analysis, who question whether different types of colleges have different impacts, have defined "type" of college in different ways. Most have approached this issue using conventional classifications (public and private; technical, liberal arts, teachers college, and so on; university or college; church-related or secular). More recently, however, there have been attempts to classify colleges in dimensions that cut across the traditional categories and thereby give a more refined and analytic understanding of the impact of the college environment. Approaches that define some critical dimensions of the "climate" of a college (see Pace, 1969; Pace and Stern, 1958; Stern, 1970) or some of its structural and organizational characteristics (Boland, 1971) reflect these attempts at more analytic classification.

This increasingly complex and analytic approach is also evident in the analyses of the impact of subunits within the college and university. In studies of the impact of major fields, most approaches have looked at the traditional departmental divisions and classifications, such as social science, physical science, and humanities. But there have been attempts to arrive at more conceptual dimensions relevant in studies of impact on students — for example, a categorization in terms of the extent to which faculty in the department or division have "moral" or "normative" goals in their relations with their students (Gamson, 1966; Vreeland & Bidwell, 1966).

There are obvious problems in approaching a phenomenon as complex as the four-year college experience and attempting to analyze the particular aspects of the experience that had special relevance for a given type of student change. Moreover, regardless of the level of complexity of one's attempt to tie change to characteristics of the college environment, all such efforts suffer from a common problem: the need to control the selection factor that brings different kinds of students to different colleges and to different programs and experiences within any given college. This problem is particularly critical, since students who choose different colleges and different environments within college differ in those very dimensions in which we are particularly interested in measuring impact and change. If, for example, we want to measure the impact of college on a student's intellectual orientations, we find that the colleges and the subenvironments within a college most strongly oriented intellectually attract students who already are highly intellectually oriented. When students emerge from the college experience with stronger intellectual orientations, we therefore have to separate the impact of their experience from the fact that they started more oriented in this direction.

Many attempts have been made to deal with this selection problem. At the simplest level, one can control for initial position by comparing only those students in the different college environments who started from relatively the same position on the given characteristic whose change we are studying. At a much more complex level, very sophisticated statistical techniques have been developed to control not only for initial position on the particular variable of interest, but for many other relevant factors that distinguish people who enter the different environments.

Astin's work (Astin, 1963, 1970a; Astin and Panos, 1969) is particularly representative of this approach, and a number of current studies of college impact tend to use some variant of the "input-output" model that he has developed most extensively. (*Input* represents the characteristics of students at the time of entering college, and *output* represents their characteristics at graduation.) The principle of the Astin approach involves computing an expected output on the basis of a large number of relevant characteristics at entrance. This expected output is subtracted from the actual output, giving a *residual output.* The residual-output scores represent a possible effect of the college over and above the effect of relevant entering characteristics. These residual scores can then be related to measures of different college characteristics to see what kinds of college characteristics are relevant to what kinds of college output.[3]

It is beyond the scope of this discussion to go into the complicated methodological and statistical problems involved in the measurement of college impact, except to point out that no method provides a perfect solution to these issues.[4] The more sophisticated methods now being used will help avoid some of the cruder errors of earlier studies and will be more helpful in suggesting some of the refined relationships between college characteristics and impact. But it is important to keep in mind the inherent difficulty of any attempt to break into a natural process whereby people are selecting their environments which in turn have effects on them, and to analyze the environmental impact aspect of the process.[5]

---

[3]Path analysis is an example of another complex technique advocated as a way of refining the analysis of college impact in relation to selection factors (Bidwell & Vreeland, forthcoming; Feldman, 1971; Werts, 1968).

[4]In addition to the problems of selection, the measurement of impact and change is complicated by the fact that our measures of student characteristics and values have imperfect reliability. For an excellent earlier discussion of the general problems in measuring change and some suggested approaches, see Harris (1963); for a recent discussion of these issues with particular relevance to the study of college impacts see Astin (1970*b*).

[5]In a few instances, studies have been done that handle the problem of selection by approaching the experimental ideal of randomly assigning students to a given college experience, or, at least, among those who wanted the experience, randomly determining those who did or did not receive it. It is significant that in these instances where the selection factor was minimized, the results suggest that the experience does have an impact. Thus Brown (1968) demonstrated the impact on students of being assigned to a residence hall that had predominantly science or humanities majors. Siegel and Siegel (1957) showed that freshman students who drew lucky numbers enabling them to move into the "high-status" residences they desired decreased less in authoritarianism than those students who wanted to move but had to remain in the same dormitories during their sophomore years. Newcomb and his associates (1970) showed that students entering a new residential college at the University of Michigan changed more during their freshman year, on such issues as cultural sophistication and liberalism, than a control group consisting of a random sample of eligible applicants to the residential college who were rejected only for reasons of space and subsequently entered the regular liberal arts program at the university. An interesting commentary on the difficulty of obtaining "perfect" controls in a natural setting is suggested by the fact that the randomly selected control group in the Newcomb study turned out to be different from the residential college entrants on some very relevant selection characteristics, so that experimental and control groups were no longer exactly comparable on all relevant entrance characteristics. Part of the reason for this seems to be that once they were not accepted by the residential college, a number of applicants decided not to go to the university but chose a small liberal arts college instead. This meant that those rejectees who decided to take the conventional liberal arts program in the large university were biased on just those characteristics that influence the decision to choose a small college environment.

The Impact of Different Kinds of Colleges

When we turn first to the studies that have focused on the college as a whole as the unit of analysis, they provide limited data on the question of whether different types of colleges have different impacts. In spite of the voluminous number of studies on college students and college change, very few have been cross-institutional in nature, comparing the changes of students in different types of institutions. Most of the research has been the product of individual professors, with limited resources, studying the available students in their own institutions. Furthermore, when cross-institutional data are available, they are mainly confined to demonstrating that there is a relationship—a congruence or "fit"—between characteristics of students and the institutions they attend. Studies have rarely gone beyond this to suggest the extent to which this congruence represents college impact over and above the factor of selection.

Current research on college impact is focusing more on cross-institutional comparisons and systematic attempts to analyze the relationship of college characteristics to student change. Ten years from now we are likely to have more refined answers to our question of the different impact of colleges.

While relatively few in number, the studies that have been done on a cross-institutional basis are, however, consistent in suggesting that the changes in student values we noted in the preceding section seem to occur at all types of institutions. A number of studies of cross-sectional design (that is, comparing freshmen and seniors at one point in time) make this point. For example, an early study by Nelson (1938) demonstrated that seniors were less politically conservative than freshmen in strikingly different types of schools, varying from state universities to very fundamentalist religious institutions. More conclusive is the evidence from a few longitudinal studies that followed the same students through their college years. The Trent and Medsker study (1968), previously cited for its comparison of college attenders and nonattenders, also compared students in different types of institutions: public, private nonsectarian, and private religious colleges and universities. In all six types of institutions, they found that the students shifted in their scores on social maturity (their measure of the nonauthoritarian syndrome) between their freshman and senior years. Data from a study of eight colleges conducted by the Berkeley Center for the Study of Higher Education (Feldman and Newcomb, 1969, **2,** p. 23) indicate that students at all eight colleges (varying from

Antioch and Reed to a religious institution) increased in their civil libertarian attitudes.

A recent study reported by Chickering (1970) presents rather dramatic evidence on this issue. In a longitudinal study, Chickering followed the same students from 1965 to 1969 in 12 small colleges that varied greatly in their goals, climate, rules, teaching, and value orientations of their faculty. Given the factor of selection, these colleges drew to their campuses very different types of students, their differences consistent with the various environments of the institutions and therefore serving to reinforce the differential climates. Despite this great diversity, Chickering noted a great deal of commonality in the changes students underwent:

But despite these dramatic differences among the institutions and among the students attending them, when the 1965 freshmen who were ready to graduate in 1969 were re-tested, several major areas of change were found at virtually all the colleges: increased autonomy, increased awareness of emotions and impulses and increased readiness to express them, increased personal integration, increased aesthetic sensitivity and interest in the arts and humanities, increased tolerance for ambiguity and complexity, increased religious liberalism, and decreased concern for material possessions and practical achievement. These changes occur at highly organized institutions with numerous regulations and close adult supervision. They also occurred at a "student centered" college with little overt structure, few regulations and minimal adult supervision. At two traditional colleges—one poor and relatively unknown operating with limited facilities, the other wealthy, prestigious with ample facilities and resources—similar changes occurred. Similar changes also occurred at two nontraditional colleges, one emphasizing independent studies and flexible programming developed by students themselves, the other with a highly structured curriculum using many required courses and a complex system of comprehensive examinations. These changes occurred among very liberal students and very conservative ones, among "authoritarians" and "anti-authoritarians," among the activists and the alienated as well as among the silent majority and the apathetic (Chickering, 1970, p. 2).

Given the data that suggest an impact common to all institutions of higher education, the question remains whether certain types of institutions have greater impact than others, and whether this greater impact is consistent with the dominant purposes and "climates" of the colleges. Here the evidence and interpretations at first glance seem somewhat mixed. Astin, by using a technique that enables him to control for many selection factors, has suggested that the great differences observed in seniors in different institutions can be attributed largely to selection factors, and that there is minimal evidence that the particular type of college one goes to makes a significant difference—at least when the student "output" is in the area of intellectual and academic achievement and aspirations (Astin, 1962, 1963). Chickering (1970) has noted the interesting paradox that, because of selection factors, one sometimes finds that absolute change on some measures of attitudes and values is actually greater in those institutions stressing these values *less* than in those institutions where these values form a dominant part of the institutional climate. The latter colleges attract students who already score so high on that value that they have much less "room to move" than the students attending the former colleges. This seems to lead to a conclusion that "the best colleges have the least effect" (Chickering, 1971).

In a contrary interpretation, Feldman and Newcomb (1969) have concluded that the data suggest that, in most cases, one finds an accentuation of the initial differences that originally bring students to the different schools. For example, not only will students who are more politically liberal be attracted to schools with a predominantly liberal political climate, but such students will increase in liberalism more than the less liberal students who chose colleges with a less politically liberal atmosphere. Feldman and Newcomb (1969) propose accentuation as a very general principle applying not only to the impact of different colleges but to the impact of the different subenvironments within an institution:

Whatever the characteristics of an individual that selectively propel him toward particular educational settings—going to college, selecting a particular one, choosing a certain academic major, acquiring membership in a particular group of peers—those same characteristics are apt to be reinforced and extended by the experiences incurred in those selected settings (Feldman & Newcomb, 1969, p. 333).

While at first glance Chickering and Feldman and Newcomb seem to arrive at completely contradictory conclusions, the contradiction is largely resolved in the further analysis that Chickering conducted with his data. Since selection factors produced the paradox that colleges with a dominant value in a given area sometimes showed less impact on that value, Chickering attempted to control for these factors. In a further analysis of the data of six of the colleges in his sample, Chickering looked at the changes of only those students who started as entering freshmen with similar scores on the particular characteristics he was measuring. Although his results must be qualified by the fact that this sharply reduced the number of cases in some of his schools, the findings do suggest that when this elementary control is introduced, and we look only at students comparable in their initial position on a given characteristic, the paradox is resolved. Change in that characteristic is consistent, rather than inconsistent, with the dominant value-climate of the school (Chickering, 1970). While Chickering did not find accentuation in the literal sense, his conclusions are similar to those of Feldman and Newcomb that the dominant climate of a school not only attracts students with certain characteristics, but has a greater impact on those same characteristics.

Nor is this conclusion necessarily contradicted by the earlier findings of Astin that when one controls for many entrance factors, the differential impact of different colleges is minimal. Astin reached this conclusion in his earlier work on student outputs of academic-intellectual achievement and aspirations. Astin found greater effects of the characteristics of different colleges in a study of college impact on vocational choices (Astin and Panos, 1969). He has also found evidence of the impact of differential college characteristics in his current work where he is more concerned with college effects on the kinds of *value* orientations that have been the major concern in this chapter (Astin, 1970a).

In general, then, while cross-institutional studies are still relatively few, the data do seem to suggest two tentative conclusions: one, that the college experience seems to have some impact on student values regardless of the nature of the college, and two, that within this general tendency, there seem to be differential effects that are consistent with the dominant climates of the different colleges. The second of these conclusions is not surprising, since we would expect a person to be affected by the values predominating in the social and cultural environment that he is involved in over a four-year period. Perhaps more surprising is the suggestion that some "liberalizing" change occurs regardless of the college's predominant values. As Jacob noted, these changes in college are consistent with some of the movements in American society generally over the past several decades. But the changes seem to be greater among college students than amoung young people not going to college; even Jacob suggested that college seems to have some intensifying and facilitative effect with respect to these cultural influences.

It is not obvious why college should have such a facilitative effect.

There does not seem to be an automatic broadening of horizons that comes with a college education, since as we have noted, a college education does not seem to have opened the older generations to the growing liberalization of recent years. It is likely, also, that more is involved than bringing together large numbers of people undergoing similar change processes, since one would not likely find the same degree of change among young people between the ages of 17 and 21 gathered in other institutional settings, for example the military. Part of the reason for a common effect may reflect the fact that the American college in recent years has been an institution that encouraged and legitimized self-confrontation and the questioning and reevaluation of one's values, and the *current* values of society, and that this has been true to some extent regardless of the nature of the college.[6]

The Impact of Different Within-College Experiences The interest in relating student impact to different types of colleges has been paralleled by an interest in delineating different environments within a given institution and studying their different impacts. Studies have compared students in several formal subunits of colleges and universities, particularly department and major field divisions. They have also compared students in different residential settings (such as "Greeks" and "Independents") and, in the past decade, various informal campus groupings, particularly those reflecting peer groups and peer subcultures.

It is beyond the scope of this chapter to examine the research literature in these areas. An excellent summary of the research and discussion of the socialization issues involved in interpreting these differential effects is provided in chapters 6, 7 and 8 of Feldman and Newcomb (1969). In general, the research on the different impact of different subenvironments suffers from the same limitations and problems as the research on the impact of different colleges: there are few studies that have systematically compared the attitudes and values of the students in the different environments. Moreover, only a handful of these has had an adequate longitudinal design enabling one to examine the issue of impact over and above selection factors.

Generally, the research literature does suggest a number of consistent relationships between certain subinstitutional divisions and student attitudes and values. This varies somewhat according to the nature of the attitude as well as the particular subenvironments

[6]We are indebted to Zelda F. Gamson for pointing up this issue.

being compared. Findings from different studies seem to be somewhat more consistent in the comparisons among students in different major fields. For example, students in the social sciences (and, to some extent, the humanities) consistently score higher on scales of liberalism and nonauthoritarianism than students in the natural sciences, business, and engineering. Findings comparing students in different residences are less consistent, reflecting the fact that conventional categories like "Greeks" and "Independents" contain much intra-institutional and inter-institutional variation.

Even granting some inconsistency, there is, however, evidence of considerable variation between students in different environmental settings. Less clear is the extent to which these findings reflect different environmental impact rather than selection. Feldman and Newcomb (1969, Ch. 6) interpret the data on major fields as evidencing the same accentuation they noted in contrasting the effects of different colleges. In their interpretation, given fields not only attract students with certain characteristics, but also provide an environment that has special impact on those same characteristics. Feldman and Newcomb, however, point out that this can be affected by other characteristics of the college. (For example, they feel accentuation would occur more often in a large heterogeneous university than in a small homogeneous college where institutionwide impact might override departmental differences.) Feldman and Newcomb also feel that the evidence for accentuation is more consistent in studies of the impact of major fields than of other types of subenvironments such as different residential arrangements.

One problem in trying to find consistency across institutions between a given kind of subenvironment and its impact on students is that impact often depends on the complex interrelationships between the institution and the subenvironment. For example, in one institution a deviant subculture might see its function as encapsulating its members from the dominant pressures of the university and, hence, reinforcing the process of accentuation. In another institution the same kind of deviant subculture might maintain or foster interaction with the university, and its members might be more affected by the institutionwide normative pressures. In general, then, the issues are too complex and the evidence too tentative to emerge yet with any consistent generalizations on the differential impacts of different subenvironments and the conditions that maximize differential effects.

In terms of the broader concern of this volume, we are interested in studies of different subenvironments because tying impact to different institutional characteristics suggests the *process* by which college has an impact. The delineation of subenvironmental differences does not, in itself, provide an understanding of this process. One must go beyond the statement that student change is related to major field, to an analysis of the relation of change to different departmental characteristics — for example, the curriculum content, the value climate, and the patterns of faculty and peer interactions. But documenting the existence of environmental differences is at least the first step in proceeding from a statement that college has an effect to some understanding of the meaning of this effect.

Refined analytic studies systematically relating impacts to environmental characteristics are more characteristic of current, unpublished research in this area than they are of the research available in the literature. There are, however, a few landmark studies that have attempted to systematically investigate, in an empirical quantitative study, the process by which the college environment influences a student's values. This research has tended to view college impact as a socialization and social influence process rather than a more intellectual process (see, for example, Newcomb, 1943; Newcomb et al., 1967; Vreeland and Bidwell, 1965, 1966; Wallace, 1966). The predominant framework has been to view value change as a process of taking on the values of faculty and particularly peers, rather than as an intellectual integration of the information and content material to which one is exposed in college. For example, Bidwell and Vreeland (forthcoming, and Vreeland and Bidwell, 1966) in their study of the impact of departments, focused on the faculty-student relationships and the issue of whether or not faculty see their role in "moral" terms, with values an important aspect of what they are teaching. Particularly striking are the studies (e.g., Newcomb et al., 1967; Wallace, 1966) that have not only focused on social interaction but have stressed peer interaction to the exclusion of the faculty (to some extent because the researcher was interested in student attitudes and values where peers have particular relevance, rather than intellectual and vocational outcomes where faculty are more relevant).

In focusing on social influences, particularly peer interactions, research studies have chosen a very crucial aspect of the influence process in college. There is no disagreement with Feldman and Newcomb's conclusion that

... there are few observers of undergraduate education in America who doubt that colleges' impacts, insofar as they occur at all, are in one way or another mediated, enhanced, or counteracted by peer group influences (Feldman & Newcomb, 1969, p. 222).

But it is interesting to speculate why the concern of the systematic, quantitative researcher on process has focused so predominantly on this issue. In reviewing the research literature, one is struck by the richness of the peer-influence studies in contrast to the lack of studies that have imaginatively attempted to study the impact of the curriculum or other aspects of the college environment as an intellectual experience.

To some extent, this may reflect the accident that the major systematic quantitative research in this area has been the work of sociologists and social psychologists, like Newcomb, Bidwell, Wallace and their associates, who have naturally focused on socialization and social influence processes. To some extent, it may be that socialization processes are easier to capture in quantitative research or that the influence of other aspects of the educational process are more elusive and difficult to quantify. But it also undoubtedly reflects the conviction on the part of close observers of the college scene that the major impact of college is as a socializing experience.

If the focus on peer-socialization influences represents an overly exclusive perspective, it has perhaps been encouraged by the fact that the major research on such influences has consisted of intensive studies within a single institution. Since they could not compare the effects of different institutions, these studies focused on the differential effects of various subcultural environments within the same institution and the ways in which these different environments mediate, support, and counteract the general institutional influences. To some extent, this may have led to an underevaluation of the impact of the total institution and the general educational experience it presents to its students, compared to what they might have received in another institution. As research on student impact moves toward multi-institutional designs, where characteristics of subcultural peer environments and the nature of peer and faculty-student interactions can be viewed in the context of other institutional characteristics, we may be able to get a better perspective on the role that social influence processes play in the value-changes that students undergo.

By its nature, a review of the college-impact literature relates to the impact of American colleges of the past several decades. These studies are obviously relevant to the cross-sectional survey data reviewed in the later chapters of this monograph, since these also reflect the extended impact of the colleges of the past. More at issue is how relevant these studies may be for the colleges and students of the future, particularly as college education becomes available to larger proportions of the American population.

While no systematic projections can be made, two sets of data may have some relevance: what does existing research tell us about the impacts of college on the students who will be more and more represented in the colleges of the future, students from less privileged socioeconomic backgrounds, students with lower academic performance, students with more vocational orientations in their college goals; and what do the data tell us about the impacts of the colleges, like community colleges, that are particularly addressed to the needs of these students?

Turning first to the data on the impact of college on students of different socioeconomic background and academic preparation, they suggest that the kinds of changes we have discussed in this chapter occur for students in all economic and academic levels. The Trent and Medsker study (1968) previously cited presents striking evidence on this issue. They divided their large population of high school graduates into high, medium, and low groups on socioeconomic status and on academic ability as measured by the Scholastic Aptitude Test. They noted some relationship between these characteristics and the students' nonauthoritarianism (as measured by their scores on the social maturity scale). Students lower in socioeconomic background and those lower in academic ability tended to be somewhat more authoritarian. But when tested four years later, all students had increased on the social maturity scale to about the same degree; that is, students low in socioeconomic background and low in academic performance increased on the social maturity scale to about the same extent as those in the medium and high classifications on both of these characteristics (Trent and Medsker, 1968, tables E-6 and E-7, pp. 305–308).

The question of whether, within this general tendency to change, those of less advantaged backgrounds and preparation change more or less than other students, is one on which evidence is still inconclusive. In reviewing the literature on this issue, Feldman and Newcomb (1969, chapter 9), suggest that some studies are consistent with an accentuation interpretation. They report that those of less advantaged backgrounds start lower on values like liberalism and nonauthoritarianism and also change less than those from a more advantaged background. Other studies are more consistent with the opposite hypothesis that, coming from backgrounds more discontinuous with what they meet in college, there is more possibility for these students to change and they consequently change somewhat more than do those from a more advantaged background. The issue is complex, and the valid interpretation probably varies with the nature of the college and its orientations toward students from divergent backgrounds. At any rate, whether students from lower socioeconomic backgrounds change more or less, changes seem to be in the same direction; and college seems to have similar impacts on students from differential backgrounds.

The picture is somewhat less clear if we look not at the background itself, but at the kinds of orientations and college goals that tend to be more prevalent among students from lower socioeconomic backgrounds. Although there is relatively little data in this area, some studies of students with different college goals suggest that students with a dominantly vocational orientation may change less than those of other orientations. In a sense, they may be less responsive to value and ideological issues not directly relevant to their vocational interest. For example, Finney (1967) showed that vocationally oriented students changed less in political liberalism than other students. A study by Miller (1959) suggests the possibility that value-change among vocationally oriented students may be particularly dependent on the college's commitment to value issues. In a cross-sectional comparison of freshmen and seniors, Miller found that intellectually oriented seniors were more pro-civil rights than intellectually oriented freshmen in all the colleges he studied—five state colleges and four Ivy League schools. Among more vocationally oriented students, however, the freshman-senior difference occurred only at the Ivy League schools. In the atmosphere of the five state colleges, a climate less dedicated to civil rights, the vocationally oriented students did not indicate any freshman-senior difference. The data are cross-sectional and should be interpreted with caution. But they suggest that students with strong intellectual orientations may find in diverse college environments the stimulus toward change. In contrast, the vocationally oriented students may need an environment particularly involved in value issues to divert them from their strong vocational interests and make them susceptible to environmental influences in other areas.

Turning from the types of *students* going to college and looking at the types of *colleges* that will become more prevalent, the evidence generally supports the conclusions we suggested in the discussion of the impact of different colleges: namely, that there seems to be some common impact of all types of colleges, but that there is also some different impact. Looking specifically at the junior or community college, we find that these institutions have not usually been the subject of research on college impact. But available evidence suggests that students in junior colleges undergo the same kinds of changes, but to a lesser extent, as students in four-year institutions. This is true even if we compare them only with students after an experience of two years in the four-year college. For example, Plant (1962) showed that students in the four-year colleges changed more after two years on scales such as dogmatism than junior college students after a comparable period (Telford & Plant, 1963). This is consistent with the general finding from the studies on impact that there is some relationship between the value climate of a college and its impact on the students. In general, studies have shown that on issues like nonauthoritarianism and political liberalism students in junior colleges score lower than those in other institutions.

We should stress, however, that these studies on junior colleges are not necessarily relevant to future community colleges. Findings that junior college students are less politically liberal and less concerned with political ideology, generally, may become quickly dated. There are already a number of community colleges, particularly in urban areas, where ideological issues are by no means irrelevant. While there have not been studies of the impact of such institutions, we would expect it to be greater than indicated by existing research on junior colleges.

Other aspects of future colleges may affect their impact on student values. While differing in many ways, the research reviews of Jacob and Feldman and Newcomb came to the conclusion that impact is greatest in the small high-quality liberal arts college where there is considerable homogeneity of values, some commitment to values as an important aspect of the educational process, and intensive interaction in a semi-isolated residential community. There has not been enough systematic cross-institutional research to demonstrate conclusively that such colleges do indeed have greater impact. But if these conclusions are true, then it is possible that the trends colleges take in the future—greater size and heterogeneity, more commuter settings, increasing vocational rather than value commitments—may result in less of the *direct* value impact that we have discussed in this chapter. This obviously does not negate the significance of these colleges and the great impact that they can have in other areas of life, particularly in the area of vocation and career, as well as the indirect impact that follows from making broader occupational alternatives available to many people.

To summarize, then, the research suggests that the types of students increasingly going to college are receptive to the same kinds of impact as students who have more typically gone to college in the past. This is certainly true in the case of socioeconomic background and academic preparation. It is less clear concerning vocationally oriented college goals that may become increasingly significant to college students in the years ahead. The potential impact on vocationally oriented students is likely to depend on the nature of the college. In general, the extent of impact on student values is likely to depend on colleges continuing to play a role of encouraging the examination of values as one of the tasks of the college years. Any projection into the future depends not so much on changes in the characteristics of the students going to college, as on how colleges may change in response to the perceived needs of these students, as well as in response to the other forces impinging on them.

A CONCLUD- To summarize and anticipate the future chapters on the college
ING COMMENT graduate, the studies on change in college provide a background that is fairly consistent with the data from cross-sectional surveys that we will be examining.

On issues of liberalism, tolerance, open-mindedness, rationality, there is clear evidence of freshman-to-senior change, that this change is greater than it is for noncollege populations, and that the change persists into the postcollege years. This liberalization seems to reflect an impact of college generally, although it is also differentially affected by different colleges, and by different experiences within a college.

Among the interpreters of the meaning of these changes, there is also a good deal of agreement that the changes reflect, in large part, a process of social influence. Interpreters vary mainly in their attitudes about this. Jacob views it as somehow a failure of college since it does not represent a direct impact of the educational and intellectual experience per se. Katz, as a personality theorist interested in the college's potential for helping the individual student develop and grow, also sees the change as somewhat more limited than he might have hoped. Newcomb, as a social psychologist, views it in less judgmental terms as the natural process by which attitudes and values are formed and changed.

There is also a significant implication underlying these different attitudes toward the interpretation that college change is a reflection of social influence. Jacob felt this reflected a superficiality of the change; he stressed that this meant that the change was not "internalized." In a sense, Newcomb's finding in his follow-up of the Bennington women might be viewed as in agreement with Jacob's point of view, since Newcomb found that persistence of change was dependent on continued social support of attitudes. But this does not negate the fact that the women in Newcomb's study sought these social supports, chose a husband and friends conforming to their views that had changed in college, and that the changes had persisted for 20 years. Lack of internalization cannot be equated with lack of significance, since all our values and attitudes are imbedded in social and cultural networks. That one does not find basic character restructuring and deep internalization of new values may not represent a failure of college as much as a limitation on the nature of the changes that are possible after the early formative childhood years. In a thoughtful and provocative essay, Brim (1966) has suggested that it is very difficult to introduce in later life the conditions of early childhood that make value formation and internalization the natural processes of the early years. He suggests that postchildhood socialization involves different processes and effects. But this does not mean that the later processes and effects are not significant, persistent, and critical to the orientations and life-styles an individual carries into adult life. Within these limitations, it would appear that American colleges over past decades have had a significant impact on many of their students.

4. Higher Education and Economic Behavior

Burkhard Strumpel

When aspiring students and their parents speak of advantageous consequences accruing from a college education, "a good job" is most frequently mentioned (Campbell & Eckerman, 1964). It is mentioned most often by parents whose own education is less than college, and ceases to be the most important factor only among those who have a college degree and an income well above the population median. The term "a good job" covers a number of factors, of course, such as work conditions, meaningfulness, and advancement and security, but income is an obvious component.

There is quite a range of financial achievement among college-trained people, but the effect of training is probably best assessed by looking at the income and education of *family heads*. An adequate example of the size of differences is shown by figures from 1968 (Katona, Dunkelberg, Hendricks, & Schmiedeskamp, 1970). There is a clear increment at every stage of education (Tables 13 and 14).

Another type of variation concerns the kind of college attended by the college educated. There have been many attempts to rank colleges according to their quality, but Morgan and Sirageldin (1968) compared the family heads' annual earnings for groups, according to the selectivity of the college from which graduates received their degree, as assessed by Cass and Birnbaum in their Comparative Guide to American Colleges (1964). They based their indexes of quality on the percentage of applicants accepted by the college, the average test scores of recent freshmen, the ranking of recent freshmen in their high school classes, and other data related to the scholastic potential of the student body. Excluded from their analysis are those who owned a business, those with no income, and those few, extreme, high-income cases (over $50,000) that distort an average. Their results show that about three-quarters

Education of family head	Mean income in 1968	Total	Less than $3,000	$3,000 -4,999
0–5 grades	$4,000	100	52	22
6–8 grades	6,300	100	33	16
9–11 grades, some high school plus noncollege	8,820	100	17	15
12 grades, completed high school	9,480	100	6	12
Completed high school plus other noncollege	9,890	100	5	14
College, no degree	10,830	100	14	9
College, bachelor's degree	13,030	100	6	10
College, advanced or professional degree	16,460	100	3	6

TABLE 13 Total family income —within various groups (percentage distribution of families)

SOURCE: Katona et al., 1970.

from the *most selective* colleges had annual earnings in excess of $10,000 (in 1964); almost half of those with degrees from *selective* colleges reported that income, and only one-quarter from *nonselective* institutions were at that income level.

The economic consequences of education for individuals have, up to now, been measured almost exclusively in terms of earning differential between people with different educational attainment. Survey data analyzed here enable and urge that the economic impact of education on individuals be viewed in a broader perspec-

TABLE 14 Education by total family income in 1968 (percentage distribution of families)

Family income	0–5 grades	6–8 grades	9–11 grades	12 grades
Less than $3,000	21	37	17	6
$3,000–3,999	15	31	17	10
$4,000–4,999	9	18	22	18
$5,000–5,999	6	22	24	16
$6,000–7,499	5	24	19	18
$7,500–9,999	3	17	18	22
$10,000–14,999	1	11	16	21
$15,000 or more	1	8	12	14
All families	7	20	17	16

SOURCE: Katona et al., 1970.

$5,000 -7,499	$7,500 -9,999	$10,000 -14,999	$15,000 or more	Number of cases	Median
13	7	4	2	143	$2,920
19	14	13	5	410	5,170
20	17	22	9	402	7,260
18	24	29	11	415	8,940
18	20	31	12	264	9,060
12	17	31	17	329	9,610
14	13	29	28	239	11,240
6	15	31	39	109	13,120

tive. An educational revolution leaving its imprint on almost every aspect of society has been taking place in America for several decades. In addition to altering the income and wealth position of its beneficiaries, higher education has changed the readiness and ability of people to shape their material future and that of their children. It has added to job security and career prospects and has increased people's satisfaction with their jobs, their standard of living, and their expectations for the time ahead.

Higher-educated individuals not only tend to have more com-

12 plus noncollege training	Some college	College degree	Advanced degree	Total
3	12	3	1	100
10	9	7	1	100
13	10	8	2	100
9	15	6	2	100
14	9	9	2	100
13	15	8	4	100
14	19	12	6	100
11	19	22	13	100
11	14	10	5	100

mand over resources, they also are more in control of their economic situation. They are less subject to the risk of unemployment, illness, or the obsolescence of skills or experiences. They have objectively more opportunities and are subjectively better equipped, intellectually as well as motivationally, to utilize them. Moreover, they more frequently are able to plan ahead, to provide for the future, and, at any point in time, to profit from such provisions made in the past. All these changes have a bearing on how people behave in the marketplace, whether as consumers in the commodity or credit markets, or as workers, professionals, or students in the market for labor and education. But there is no analysis here of the impact of education on entrepreneurial behavior or on innovation and technical progress. Instead, the focus is the economics of the private household.

A first brief overview of the data presented here suggested that there are indeed drastic differences between educational classes in their economic status and behavior. Nevertheless, the working title of the draft, "Economic Consequences of Higher Education," was soon abandoned and replaced with a less ambitious one. To ask what part of economic behavior is "due" to higher education (in other words: How would individuals or the nation behave were there no higher education?) would be to pose a question that cannot be answered by survey research and that, moreover, is of little relevance. The educational revolution is an expression of the peculiar American culture. It is a component of socioeconomic change embedded in a host of other changes, many of which it tends to reinforce. At the same time being a symptom and agent, the revolution has a symbolic as well as instrumental, a consumptive as well as productive quality. Higher education is aspired to because it stands for a desired way of life that is all but synonymous with modern, urban, upper-middle-class living.

To choose higher education, as William H. Whyte pointed out several decades ago, means to purchase entrance billets to social advancement. Even access to middle management positions and clerical jobs nowadays tends to be reserved for college graduates. Higher education is now fairly accessible to young people of all backgrounds, and those who avail themselves of it stand to achieve greater success than those who do not. Moreover, since people usually do not begin major educational efforts once past youth, missing out initially tends to relegate the less educated to a lower socioeconomic status.

The antiegalitarian impact of much of today's higher education is a long way from the function accorded to mass education (and higher education has become mass education) by the founding fathers of the American educational philosophy. Horace Mann, the commanding figure of the early public school movement, was concerned throughout his career with the proficiency of average students. He contended that, in a republic, leaders could never far surpass the general popular level. Hence the important thing for him was not the training of elites but rather the education given the great body of the people (Cremin, 1957, pp. 23, 26). Education during most of American history was considered an instrument for socializing a heterogeneous immigrant population, the foundation of popular power, the door to opportunity, and the great equalizer in the race for success (Hofstadter, 1963, pp. 305f). According to Mary Jean Bowman (1962), the philosophy leading to the large-scale establishment of land-grant institutions of higher education is closely linked to the concept of the *undifferentiated* American. Public higher education was directed toward all crafts. "If lawyers and doctors had higher institutions to serve them, farmers and mechanics should too; weren't their callings just as dignified?" (Bowman, 1962, p. 526).

The data presented here point to the differentiating effects of modern mass higher education on economic behavior and status. This is not to deny, however, that the relatively higher welfare enjoyed by the higher educated, to a large extent, reflects a net gain for society as a whole. Education, of course, is not a zero-sum game; it does more than merely decide how an existing pool of opportunities is to be distributed. Education is an area of change where deeply rooted popular aspirations and market demand are in rare harmony with each other. A technologically ever more sophisticated economy demands more higher education as urgently as a more urbane and affluent populace does. And the ready response of Americans to the challenge of the knowledge society, as well as the ability of the economy to absorb ever higher numbers of the college educated at rising pay rates, no doubt contributed to the edge the American economy holds over other industrial economies in productivity generally, as well as in fields of intensive knowledge like electronics, cybernetics, aerospace, and industrial management.[1]

[1] For a more detailed treatment of international differences of education and their economic consequences, see Katona, Strumpel, & Zahn, 1971.

	Using unadjusted
Amount of education completed	earning rates
0–8 grades	$ 86,600
9–11 grades	91,100
12 grades	91,100
12 grades and nonacademic training	92,400
College, no degree	92,850
College, bachelor's degree	108,150
College, advanced degree	111,000

TABLE 15
Expected future earnings at age 15, discounted at 4 percent assuming 2,000 hours of work per year to age 65* (for all white, male, nonfarm heads of spending units, 1959)

* There is some evidence that the differential between those with the least amount of education and those with one or more college degrees is increasing. See Morgan & Lininger, 1964.

SOURCE: Morgan & David, 1963.

There is conclusive evidence that higher education as an investment, in the statistical average (including women, part-time workers, and persons who die during their working years), does not pay a long-term market return in monetary terms. The often-quoted figure of $100,000 as the value of a college education requires many qualifications limiting the population to which such a figure might apply. There is no question that the average lifetime earnings of college graduates exceed those of other educational categories. This is still true after allowance is made for the delay in earnings and if a discount rate is applied. Yet according to Morgan and David (1963, p. 434), who analyzed a 1959 national sample of heads of households, a college education was worth in financial terms only $17,000–$20,000 if a moderate 4 percent discount was applied (Table 15).[2] A higher discount rate would further, and considerably, depress this figure. Houthakker (1959) in an earlier paper used Census data from 1949 and valued a college education at about $11,000 (6 percent discount). Somewhat higher are recent estimates of the Bureau of the Census (1970) based on 1968 data. Using a discount rate of 5 percent, expected lifetime income for *male, year-round, full-time* workers is estimated at $128,000 for high school graduates and at $187,000 for college

[2] The present monetary value of a college education is supposed to reflect the amount a potential investor would pay today for later payoffs of higher education. The discounted payoffs therefore ought to be compared with the costs of education consisting of tuition and income foregone because of college attendance.

graduates (4 years or more), resulting in an excess for the latter of $59,000. All quoted figures seem to be subject to downward adjustment on the basis of two considerations. First, the evidence quoted is derived from surveys conducted among heads of spending units or households, the vast majority of whom are husbands in complete families. Practically all are or have been working; i.e., they turned their education into monetary gain. Yet a considerable proportion of the higher educated, primarily married women, are not in the labor force. Their education does not yield monetary returns at all comparable to that of male family heads.

Second, some of the differences in hourly earnings between educational categories may result from parental influences and other factors associated with education. Morgan and David (1963) (see Table 15) try to take into account some of them. Afterwards even income differences between high school and college graduates over a lifetime (again only moderately discounted at 4 percent) shrink to less than $15,000 (Morgan & David, 1963, p. 434).[3]

Up to this point, there is no conclusive evidence on the direction income differentials between educational categories have taken during the sixties. Available data from the Michigan surveys of consumer finances indicate that, in spite of rapidly rising educational attainment, the higher educated held their own in the income pyramid between 1958–59 and 1968–69 (Stafford, unpublished). If there was any widening or narrowing of these differences, it would have been very small.

Higher education as an investment, at least in the United States, does not support widespread, mostly exaggerated notions about its profitability in dollar terms. The contention advanced here is that the main thrust of higher education, even in the economic sphere, lies elsewhere. There is overwhelming evidence that college-educated people hold jobs and occupations that expose them to fewer risks of accidents and income losses, and are less strenuous. These jobs also depend less for success on physical capacity, and are thus more sympathetic to the aging process; they make more use of accumulated experience; offer more advancement and a continuously rising income pattern; provide more vacation rights and other fringe benefits; and generally give more comfort, psychic

---

[3] Factors introduced by the multivariate analysis were religion, personality, father's education, local labor-market conditions, past mobility, and supervisory responsibility.

TABLE 16 *Unemployment experience* (in percent)*

	Education				
	0–11 grades	*12 grades*	*College no degree*	*Bachelor's degree*	*Advanced degree*
Ever unemployed or on strike	33	· 22	14	10	2
Never	67	78	86	90	98
N	(1,028)	(579)	(251)	(209)	(60)

* Only for present or past members of the labor force as of 1964. The question was: "Have you ever been out of a job or on strike for two months or more at one time?"

SOURCE: Morgan, Sirageldin, & Baerwaldt, 1966; education categories are slightly different than those appearing in this table.

rewards, stimulation, and satisfactions. The higher educated are thus *situationally* advantaged in monetary terms as well as in terms of security and opportunity. We shall see later that they are *motivationally* better equipped in that they are more confident of being able to master their fate, more vigorous in undertaking it, and, consequently, have a clearer sense of purpose and direction. Finally they are *behaviorally* better adapted in that, by saving more, procuring their children an education, purchasing housing and durables to a larger extent, they provide for the future as well as profit from their own and their parents' provisions in the past. Again, most of these secondary economic consequences of higher education may not be attributable to education alone. Some can be considered a concomitant of the occupational choice. Yet the choice of an occupation depends largely on earlier educational attainment, which leads logically to the choice in most cases.[4]

Studies provide evidence of situational advantages. Table 16[5] indicates clearly that involuntary absence (strike or unemployment) from the job, which almost invariably means loss of income, was experienced by more than one-third of a low educational group, almost one-fourth of high school graduates, but by only 12 percent of holders of bachelor degrees and just one out of fifty holders of advanced degrees. Recent illness or unemployment (in the last 12 months) struck a mere 12 percent of the college graduates,

[4] Occupation, in this model, plays the role of an intervening variable. The effect of education on occupation is obvious and well established. See Morgan, David, Cohen, & Brazer (1962).

[5] Figures in this and subsequent tables, if not otherwise noted, are based on a reanalysis of data collected in 1965. See Morgan, Sirageldin, & Baerwaldt (1966).

TABLE 17
Loss of work
time due to
illness,
unemployment,
or strike* (in
percent)

	Education				
	0–11 grades	12 grades	College, no degree	Bachelor's degree	Advanced degree
Loss of work time	29	23	18	12	11
No loss	63	77	82	87	89
Not ascertained	8	0	0	1	0
N	(780)	(535)	(215)	(184)	(56)

* Only for members of labor force in 1964. The question was: "How many weeks were there last year when you weren't working because of illness or unemployment?"
SOURCE: Morgan, Sirageldin, & Baerwaldt, 1966; education categories are slightly different than those appearing in this table.

compared to one-fifth of high school graduates and one-third of those with less education (Table 17). Although lower-educated members of the labor force are on the average older and therefore more likely to have experienced unemployment, there is no doubt that the more generous rules and regulations applied to professional and managerial personnel (sick leave, insurance schemes, and easier, more secure jobs) are the main reasons for the differences reflected in these figures.

Higher-educated people, mainly by virtue of their specialization, exhibit a more continuous, less erratic job history. This certainly is reflective of the greater job security enjoyed by them and of the higher demand for their services.[6] Dead-end careers are less frequent among them, and the need to start all over again arises much less frequently (Table 18). Furthermore, Morgan and his colleagues (Morgan, David, Cohen & Brazer, 1962, pp. 350f.) found in 1960 that the chance of finding alternative employment was rated good by 67 percent of college graduates, 50 percent of high school graduates with or without some college, but by only 30 percent of those who had not completed high school.[7] These answers, regardless of the extent they may be based on perceptions or objective conditions, have to be seen in conjunction with the data on job stability in Table 18. The higher educated are less

[6] Although statistical data about the recent layoffs of scientists and engineers are not available, there is little doubt that, even in the present recession, jobs of college-educated, as a whole, have again proven to be relatively more stable than those of less-educated workers.

[7] The wording of the question was: "If you should lose your present job, what would you say were your chances of finding another job that paid about the same?"

TABLE 18
Job mobility*
(in percent)

	Education				
	0–11 grades	12 grades	College, no degree	Bachelor's degree	Advanced degree
Many different jobs and occupations	41	34	37	24	16
Many different jobs, but same occupation	14	17	11	16	13
Few jobs in same occupation	44	48	49	58	71
Not ascertained	1	1	3	2	
N	(1,040)	(589)	(254)	(209)	(61)

* Only those who have ever worked as of 1964. The question was: "Have you had a number of different kinds of jobs, or have you mostly worked in the same occupation you started in, or what?"

subject to the common hazards of occupational life, less forced to endure unsatisfactory pay rates and human-relations discomforts, and thus are more able to control their working life.

The preceding differences in job characteristics would suffice to explain higher levels of satisfaction experienced by the higher educated, but there are many more. Table 19 shows that the chance for physical and psychic regeneration through three or more weeks of vacation—considered so important by doctors—was open in 1964 to more than half of the holders of advanced college degrees, 45 percent of the holders of bachelor's degrees in selective colleges, but only to every fourth high school graduate without college and to a mere 14 percent of those with less education—of which 43 percent had no vacations at all.

Chances for promotion are judged about twice as frequently

TABLE 19 *Weeks of vacation in 1964* (in percent)*

	Education					
	0–11 grades	12 grades	College, no degree	Bachelor's, nonselective college	Bachelor's, selective college	Advanced degree
No vacation	43	25	26	16	16	11
1–2 weeks	35	50	42	50	39	33
3 or more weeks	22	25	32	34	45	51
N	(701)	(517)	(205)	(89)	(84)	(55)

* Only those who worked in 1964. The question asked was: "How many weeks of vacation did you take last year?"

TABLE 20 *Chance for promotion* (in percent)*

	Education				
	0–11 grades	*12 grades*	*College, no degree*	*Bachelor's degree*	*Advanced degree*
Respondent ranks chance for promotion excellent or good, is already at the top of firm, or owns it	24	44	53	63	66

Only those in labor force in 1964. The question was: "What would you say are your chances for promotion or getting ahead in the kind of work you are doing now?"

as excellent or good by college graduates as by those with less than a high school education (Table 20). The frequency of optimistic career expectations among those who completed high school is in the middle of the other two educational classifications.

The higher educated have more opportunities to adjust their actual workload to the preferred one. While the lower echelons in the educational hierarchy are more frequently concerned about the availability of gainful employment, this is much less so for college graduates (Table 21). One-third of those with only high school education or less would like to work more if they would be paid for it. This figure decreases continuously with higher education and finally drops to 15 percent of those with an advanced college degree.

We will try to indicate how situational differences and their perceptions are translated into concerns, hopes, fears, and satisfactions. What are the values people have in mind when they

TABLE 21 *Preference for more or less work* (in percent)*

	Education				
	0–11 grades	*12 grades*	*College, no degree*	*Bachelor's degree*	*Advanced degree*
Would like to work more	38	37	29	28	15
No change	34	36	41	40	46
Would like to work less	14	13	14	16	11
Not ascertained	14	14	16	16	28
N	(694)	(512)	(202)	(172)	(54)

Only those in labor force in 1964. The question was: "Some people would like to work more hours a week if they could be paid for it. Others would prefer to work fewer hours a week even if they earned less. How do you feel about this?"

SOURCE: Morgan, Sirageldin, & Baerwaldt, 1966; education categories are slightly different than those appearing in this table.

evaluate their jobs or occupation? Obviously, several criteria are applied at the same time: income, security, satisfaction, enough leisure, and others. Still, it is of interest to learn about differences in the saliency of these goals. Are immediate or deferred, material or nonmaterial gratifications foremost in people's minds? Is a good job considered most of all a means of making as much money as possible, or a long-term, secure base of existence, or primarily a meaningful, satisfactory activity?

The saliency of the different goals most probably reflects their urgency. Those afraid of unemployment will rate job security high. He who is fairly satisfied with the amount of income received and has a secure, steady job will raise his sights to nonmaterial aspects of the job, like the satisfaction it provides. Seen from this vantage point, an impressive correlation between higher education and preoccupation with nonmaterial job characteristics emerges in the proportion of people who say "work is important, gives feeling of accomplishment." Two-thirds of the holders of advanced degrees, 40 percent of other college graduates, but only between 10 and 20 percent of those with high school education or less, can afford to judge a job mainly on nonmaterial payoffs. For the higher educated, this correlation indicates a high degree of complacency or satisfaction with the more utilitarian aspects of their job like security, income, and working time.

While less-educated workers show less concern with the nonmaterial aspects of the job, they give security-oriented answers more frequently. Fifty-eight percent of high school graduates and sixty-two percent of those with less education consider a steady income or the absence of the risk of job loss the most important ingredient of a good job (Table 22). The same answers were given by less than 30 percent of the holders of bachelor's degrees and by only 18 percent of the holders of advanced degrees. There is little difference between the educational groups with respect to the preference for maximizing one's income or for career advancement.

Given the easier access to desirable jobs for the college educated, it is hardly surprising that actual job satisfaction is highly correlated with education. In a survey conducted in 1967 (Mueller, 1969), a cross section of the American labor force was asked whether they enjoyed their work or whether they considered it drudgery. Table 23 shows that nearly 90 percent of the college graduates said, without qualification, that they enjoyed their

TABLE 22 *Job characteristic preferences, 1964* (in percent)*

	Education				
	0–11 grades	12 grades	College, no degree	Bachelor's degree	Advanced degree
High income	9	9	11	11	7
Security†	63	58	40	31	18
Meaningful, interesting activity	13	18	30	40	67
Other	15	15	19	18	8
N	(1,084)	(595)	(259)	(111)	(61)

* The question was: "Would you please look at this card and tell me which thing on this list about a job (occupation) you would most prefer, which comes next, which is third, and so forth?" The categories were: Income is steady; Income is high; There's no danger of being fired or unemployed; Working hours are short, lots of free time; Chances for advancement are good; The work is important, gives a feeling of accomplishment.

† No danger of being fired or unemployed and steady income.

work. This is true of only 70 percent in the lower educational categories. The less educated often gave pro-con answers—in some ways they enjoyed their job, in others they disliked it.

A study concerning automation contains evidence testifying to the higher adaptability of college-trained workers to this kind of change. In response to the study question ("In general would you say the automation is a good thing for people doing your kind of work, or does it cause problems, or doesn't it make any difference?") attitudes became more favorable with increases in formal education (Table 23). College-educated workers not only use automated equipment more frequently than others; in the majority of cases, they seem to like this development. They profit more from innovations in their pay, other remuneration, and job satisfaction. To those with less education, automation is more often threatening, probably because the less skilled and less complex jobs are more easily taken over by machines than those of more highly educated members of the labor force. Even in the lower-educated groups, however, the majority hold that automation makes no difference or is a good thing. There is no evidence whatever that people with a good deal of formal education feel that the increasing use of machines in connection with their work and the increasing capability of the machines they work with are incompatible with their education (Mueller, 1969).

As a result of the pattern of rising incomes and greater security and satisfaction, there is a significantly more favorable perception

<table>
<tr><td rowspan="3">**TABLE 23**
Education and worker's attitudes toward their jobs and equipment* (in percent)</td><td></td><td colspan="4">*Education*</td></tr>
</table>

	0–11 grades	*12 grades*	*College, no degree*	*College degree*
Job is:				
Enjoyable	70	78	82	89
Pro-con	22	16	14	8
Durdgery	7	4	3	2
Not ascertained	1	2	1	1
Automation is:				
Good	24	36	43	47
Pro-con	3	3	3	3
Bad	15	11	8	4
Makes no difference	56	48	43	42
Not ascertained	2	2	3	4
N	(975)	(854)	(407)	(383)

* The questions were: "On the whole, do you feel that the work on your present job is drudgery, or is it all right, or do you enjoy your work?" and "In general, would you say that automation is a good thing for people doing your kind of work, or does it cause problems or doesn't it make any difference?"

SOURCE: Mueller, 1969.

of the personal economic situation (Table 24) and, although less self-evident, of the economy as a whole. Table 24 shows that of the college graduates in a study, 46 percent described themselves as better off than a year ago, while only 20 percent of the lowest educational category did; respectively, 64 percent and 39 percent felt better off than 4 years ago. Forty-seven percent of the college graduates expected improvements in the next 12 months compared to 19 percent of those without a high school diploma; 59 and 25 percent, respectively, expected to be better off in 4 years. The percentages for high school graduates in all cases were somewhere in the middle. If the same comparisons are made within age-education categories, differences tend to be somewhat larger within the younger than in the older groups, reflecting the extremely favorable attitude of college graduates in the first stages of their career.

Less straightforward is the significantly more optimistic and confident posture college graduates tend to take toward the economy as a whole. The lower educated frequently take a gloomier view of the future course of the economy. In one study (Table 25), 43 percent of the college graduates expected good times for the next 12 months, compared to 38 percent of high school graduates,

TABLE 24 Perceptions and expectations of personal economic situation, 1970 (in percent)	Education		
	Less than 12 grades	High school diploma; college, no degree	College degree
*Better off than one year ago:**			
Under 35 years	35	50	56
35–54	20	35	47
55 or older	16	20	20
All respondents	20	37	46
Better off than four years ago:†			
Under 35 years	62	66	76
35–54	51	60	64
55 or older	26	52	33
All respondents	39	55	64
Expect to be better off in one year:‡			
Under 35 years	46	60	65
35–54	27	32	42
55 or older	7	17	20
All respondents	19	40	47
Expect to be better off in four years:§			
Under 35 years	52	78	75
35–54	38	48	62
55 or older	9	17	10
All respondents	25	53	59
Number of cases:			
Under 35 years	(82)	(250)	(72)
35–54	(184)	(260)	(72)
55 or older	(294)	(149)	(30)
All respondents	(560)	(662)	(175)

* The question was: "Would you say that you and your family are better off or worse off financially than you were a year ago?"

† The question was: "Now thinking back four years, would you say that you people are better off or worse off financially than you were then?"

‡ The question was: "Now looking ahead, do you think a year from now you people will be better off financially, or worse off, or just about the same as now?"

§ The question was: "And four years from now, do you expect that you and your family will be better off, worse off, or just about the same as now?"

SOURCE: *1970 Survey of Consumer Finances.*

and 30 percent of the lowest educational group. Concerning long-term expectations, 34, 23, and 13 percent, respectively, felt the next five years would bring essentially favorable economic condi-

		Education	
TABLE 25 Expectations concerning the economy, 1970* (in percent)	*Less than 12 grades*	*High school diploma; some college, no degree*	*College degree*
One-year business expectations:			
Good times	30	38	43
Pro-con	8	8	9
Bad times	38	38	36
Depends, not ascertained	24	16	12
Five-year business expectations:			
Good times	13	23	34
Pro-con	9	11	18
Bad times	52	44	31
Depends, not ascertained	26	22	17
N	(560)	(662)	(175)

* The questions were: "Now turning to business conditions in the country as a whole, do you think that during the next 12 months we'll have good times financially, or bad times, or what?" and "Looking ahead, which would you say is more likely—that in the country as a whole we'll have continuous good times during the next 5 years or so, or that we will have periods of widespread unemployment or depression, or what?"
SOURCE: *1970 Survey of Consumer Finances.*

tions. Bad conditions were foreseen by 52 percent of the lower educational group and stratum, 22 percent of the high school graduates, but by only 17 percent of the college graduates.

This is a clear example of how a personal frame of reference is transferred to broader cognitive phenomena. Those who view their own economic situation as favorable tend to take an optimistic view of the economy as well. The chain of causation most probably works in both directions. If one looks at changes in economic behavior of the masses during the last two decades, two powerful trends stand out: the increased frequency of higher education and

TABLE 26 Labor-force participation rates, all females age 20–64, USA	*Year*	*White*	*Nonwhite*	*Married**
	1951	31.5	41.1	25.2
	1960	34.1	41.2	30.5
	1966	36.5	44.1	35.4

* Married, spouse present.
SOURCES: *Yearbook of Labor Statistics,* various years, and U.S. Department of Labor, 1968.

the rise in labor-force participation by married women (Table 26). What impact, if any, did the former have on the latter? Three powerful incentives induce the educated wife to take up gainful employment: the higher income she can make compared to an unskilled worker; the fairly pleasant working conditions she is in a position to find; and dissatisfaction with the limitations of housework. Table 27 demonstrates the relationship between education and labor-force participation; this relationship is closely intertwined with the income situation of the household as well as with age.

Age and education are interrelated because, at the present time, those in younger age groups have had more extensive schooling than those in older groups. Nevertheless, education, particularly college education, makes a difference in the rate of working wives within age groups as well. For instance, among wives under 25 years of age, 78 percent of the college educated, 70 percent of the high school graduates, and 43 percent of those with less than high school education were employed in 1968. Differences among educational groups also existed among women between the ages of 45 and 54, although the impact of education on the rate of employment among older women appears to be less than among younger women.

It is noteworthy that, disregarding age, the more education a married woman has, the more she tends to remain in the labor force even though her husband's higher-than-average income exerts an influence in the opposite direction. Thus the stimulating effect of education on employment of college-educated women is powerful enough to more than offset the opposite effect of the relatively high income of their husbands (Katona, Strumpel, & Zahn, 1971, p. 140). Data from 1964 contain a more detailed classification of the higher-educated groups. Table 28 shows that with college-educated wives, there is a strong association between education and labor-force participation, ranging from 53 percent among the women with only some college to 75 percent of those with advanced degrees.

Since behavior is subject to the pressures of reality and is therefore only partly dependent on what people prefer to do, there is no one-to-one relationship between attitudes and behavior. Nevertheless, a consideration of attitudes and preferences toward mothers' working outside the home throws light on the relative strength of traditions, on the one hand, and more modern attitudes

	Proportion of wives working	Proportion in subgroup

All wives	48	100
Earned income of head:†		
Under $5,000	67	18
$5,000–7,499	61	26
$7,500–9,999	52	25
$10,000–14,999	44	23
$15,000 or more	35	8
Age of wife:		
Under 25	64	13
25–34	54	25
35–44	50	20
45–54	54	19
55–64	40	13
65 or older	12	10
Education of wife:		
0–11 grades	41	36
12 grades	51	42
Some college or more	56	21
Age and education of wife:		
Under age 25:		
0–11 grades	43	3
12 grades	70	6
Some college or more	78	3
Age 25–34:		
0–11 grades	53	6
12 grades	51	11
Some college or more	59	7
Age 35–44:		
0–11 grades	53	7
12 grades	49	9
Some college or more	50	4
Age 45–54:		
0–11 grades	50	7
12 grades	55	9
Some college or more	60	3

TABLE 27
Labor-force participation of wives, 1968* (in percent)

* The question was: "Did your wife do any work for money in 1968?"
† Heads in the labor force.
  SOURCE: Katona, Strumpel, & Zahn, Table C-3, p. 223.

			Education of wife		
TABLE 28 *Education and labor-force participation of wife, 1964* (in percent)*		*0–11 grades*	*12 grades*	*College, no degree*	*Bachelor's degree*	*Advanced degree*

TABLE 28
Education and labor-force participation of wife, 1964* (in percent)

	Education of wife				
	0–11 grades	*12 grades*	*College, no degree*	*Bachelor's degree*	*Advanced degree*
Wife worked:					
Yes	39	48	53	61	75
No	61	52	47	39	25
N	(702)	(641)	(173)	(108)	(8)

* The education categories appearing in this table are slightly different than those used in the original data analysis. The question was: "Did your wife do any work for money last year?"

SOURCE: Morgan, Sirageldin, & Baerwaldt, 1966.

on the other. The matter of a married woman with children going out to work is delicate, controversial, and often determined by the attitudes of the husband. Education, as 1964 data show, is strongly associated with a favorable attitude toward working mothers (Table 29). Of household heads in the lowest educational category, 65 percent flatly denounced paid work by mothers as bad, compared to only 21 percent of heads of households with advanced degrees. Significantly, actual labor-force participation of wives, strongly dependent on the wife's education, hardly rises with the educational attainment of the husband. Husbands with higher education, although more sympathetic to working wives, receive higher incomes; here, two variables counteract (Katona, Strumpel, & Zahn, 1971, p. 144).

Higher education is associated with, if not actually producing, attitudes and behavior that facilitate adaptation to socioeconomic change even in areas not directly related to occupations. One es-

TABLE 29 *Attitude toward wife working, 1964* (in percent)*

	Education of head				
	0–11 grades	*12 grades*	*College, no degree*	*Bachelor's degree*	*Advanced degree*
Attitude toward wife working:					
Good idea	32	35	30	38	88
Pro-con	11	20	19	25	44
Bad idea	55	44	50	35	21
Not ascertained	2	1	1	2	2
N	(1,084)	(595)	(259)	(111)	(61)

The question was: "Suppose a family has children but they are all in school—would you say it is a good thing for the wife to take a job or a bad thing, or what?"

SOURCE: Reanalysis of data from the Survey Research Center, University of Michigan, 1964.

sential ingredient of adaptive behavior is what may be called a future orientation. A wise household takes future objectives, needs, and opportunities into consideration by making economic decisions about work and leisure, consumption and saving, and housing, moving, and education. The family does not live from day to day, from hand to mouth. It attempts to provide for contingencies, to minimize risks, to provide for the well-being of the next generation, even if sacrifice of present-day gratifications is required.

How does higher education affect behavior such as risk avoidance, the accumulation of reserve funds, the use of family-planning techniques, and attitudes toward, and preparation for, the higher education of children? Table 30 indicates a high correlation between risk avoidance—in this case, the use of seat belts—and

TABLE 30 *Education and risk avoidance, 1964 (in percent)*

	Education				
	0–11 grades	12 grades	College, no degree	Bachelor's degree	Advanced degree
*Index of caution and risk avoidance:**					
0–2	48	28	17	15	10
3–4	42	50	55	51	41
5–7	10	22	28	34	49
N	(1,084)	(595)	(259)	(211)	(61)
Use of seat belts† (only families with seat belts in car):					
Fastened all the time	23	29	36	37	43
Fastened part of the time	41	43	38	48	49
Fastened hardly at all	32	26	24	15	6
Not ascertained	4	2	2	0	2
N	(164)	(179)	(104)	(97)	(49)

* The index of caution and risk avoidance was constructed as follows:

Seat belts fastened all or part of the time.	1 point
Does not try new products when they first come on the market.	1 point
All family members have had polio vaccine.	1 point
Family covered by medical or hospitalization insurance.	1 point
Family has liquid reserve funds equal to at least two months of take-home income.	1 point
Head of family married and has used some method of family planning.	2 points
Head of family not married (to neutralize those ineligible for family planning).	1 point

† The questions were: "Does the car you drive have seat belts? Do you have them fastened all the time while you are driving, part of the time, or practically none of the time?"

SOURCE: Reanalysis of data from the Survey Research Center, University of Michigan, 1964.

TABLE 31 *Use of family planning, 1964* (in percent)*

	Education				
	0–11 grades	12 grades	College, no degree	Bachelor's degree	Advanced degree
Have used family planning	31	46	59	54	49
Never used family planning	63	52	35	44	49
Not ascertained	6	2	6	2	2
N	(770)	(470)	(184)	(163)	(49)

* Only for married family heads of households. Because heads of households, rather than wives, were interviewed, the proportion reporting use of family planning is probably biased downward. The education categories appearing in this table are slightly different than those used in the original data analysis. The question was: "Have you and your wife used any method to limit the number or plan the spacing of your children?"

SOURCE: Morgan, Sirageldin, & Baerwaldt, 1966.

educational attainment. Table 31 indicates a high correlation between failure to use family-planning techniques and low educational attainment: The higher proportion of respondents without high school diplomas failing to use family planning is due mainly to greater age.

Of particular interest are the attitudes toward the amount of education considered appropriate for one's children (Table 32). Here the gulf between the lowest educational category and those who have completed high school is larger than between the latter group and the college educated. Remarkably, five-sixths of those who left the educational system with a high school diploma report a past, present, or planned college education for their sons.

Here we would like to change the model—dealing so far only with simple correlations between higher education and situational characteristics, attitudes, or behavior—to introduce parents'

TABLE 32 *Education of children of family head, 1964* (in percent)*

	Education of head				
Education of children	0–11 grades	12 grades	College, no degree	Bachelor's degree	Advanced degree
Children have gone to college or presently in college or expected to go to college	49	83	90	95	100
None of the above	51	17	10	5	0
N	(900)	(482)	(187)	(152)	(40)

* The questions were: "Do you have any children in college now?" "Do you have any children who will go to college?" "Do you have any children who have already gone to college?"

SOURCE: Reanalysis of data from the Survey Research Center, University of Michigan, 1964.

education as an interacting variable. College education, in addition to affecting its immediate beneficiaries and their future as workers and consumers, may have an indirect, long-term impact on their children and their behavior and values.

In a 1965 survey, we asked respondents about their fathers' education. There were some substantial, significant differences between college graduates whose fathers were college educated and those whose fathers were not. While there was little difference in the income and wealth situation of both groups, the first-generation graduates were considerably less advanced in terms of job motivation (Table 33). They exhibited a distinct preference for working hard in exchange for material security ("steady work"). Their colleagues with a family history of higher education much more frequently considered nonmaterial characteristics ("work is important, gives feeling of accomplishment") the most crucial yardstick of a job. Men in the latter group were also much less likely to prefer more work than they were doing, which again indicates a departure from lower middle-class values stressing "hard work for hard money." Risk avoidance (apart from the risk of unemployment) for first-generation college graduates was more likely to be of only peripheral concern; e.g., seat belts were fastened regularly by only 32 percent as opposed to 51 percent of second-generation graduates.

Economists have traditionally looked at welfare primarily as meaning command over material resources. Consequently, the attempt to assess the economic impact of education has stressed the monetary payoffs. In a society where the majority of adults have jobs that sustain them and their family decently, income differences per se, although important, are only one of the appropriate criteria for measuring the welfare consequences of higher education. With rising affluence, other aspirations, such as job and income security, availability of opportunities for advancement, choices of alternatives to unsatisfactory conditions, a good working environment, and human relations gain in importance. This is indicated clearly by the particular frequency of security-oriented job preferences among the lower-middle class and satisfaction-oriented preferences among the upper-middle class. The higher educated are far ahead of their less-educated contemporaries in pursuing and realizing these qualitative goals. Given the modest monetary payoff of higher education, at least in actuarial terms, we might conclude that part of the intergroup differences in the

TABLE 33 *Intergenerational educational mobility and preferences for more work, job characteristic preferences, caution and risk avoidance, 1964 (in percent)*

	Father had some college, head has degree	Father had no college, head has degree	Head does not have college degree
Preference for more or less work (only those in labor force):			
More work	12	31	36
No change	46	39	36
Less work	16	14	14
Not ascertained	26	16	14
N	(63)	(164)	(1,418)
Highest rank given to:			
High income	12	10	9
*Security**	19	32	59
Meaningful, interesting activity	58	42	17
Other	11	16	15
N	(77)	(195)	(1,942)
Caution and risk avoidance index:			
0–1	1	3	14
2	6	12	24
3	29	24	26
4	17	27	20
5	31	21	12
6–7	16	13	4
N	(77)	(195)	(1,942)
Use of seat belts (only those owning cars with seat belts):			
Fastened all the time	51	32	29
Fastened part of the time	41	52	42
Fastened hardly at all	8	16	26
Not ascertained	0	0	3
N	(44)	(101)	(463)

* No danger of being fired or unemployed and steady income.
SOURCE: Reanalysis of data from the Survey Research Center, University of Michigan, 1964.

nonincome components of well-being are indeed the outcome of a substitution process. The higher educated can afford to accept less opulent jobs or occupations which, nevertheless, supply more security, choice of alternatives, comfort, meaningfulness, and thus, satisfaction.

Yet our data have shown that education does more for the individual than offer a more complete fulfillment of given wants, needs, and preferences. Higher education changes people and their tastes. It facilitates behavioral change not just by providing the means to do so; it affects people's goals, values, and reference groups. We found that people with college degrees much more frequently exhibit risk-avoiding behavior (as in the use of seat belts), provide for the education of their children, and accumulate reserve funds. Education opens new vistas for people. While improving the means of accomplishing their aspirations, it also raises the aspirations. In particular, education extends time horizons. Adaptive economic behavior is based on an incorporation of tomorrow's needs into today's decision making. In the knowledge society, the time lag between education, training, the gathering of experience, and its payoff in terms of career advancement and income tends to grow. Thus a household intending to raise its socioeconomic status must become increasingly able and willing to defer gratifications.

The discussion here might be considered to strengthen the case of those who see the justification for America's educational revolution and its continuation primarily in "secondary payoffs," responding to the need for a more comfortable, prosperous, secure, and meaningful existence, rather than acting merely as a device for the production of skilled manpower in exchange for monetary rewards. Unlike other basic aspects of socioeconomic change, such as bureaucratization, division of labor, agglomeration, and pollution, which are said to subjugate basic human needs to the dynamics of economic production and growth, higher education is closely geared to both the needs of economic progress and to the aspirations of the modern man.

Most changes in higher education can be viewed, for the individual educated, as beneficial in the sense of conforming to widespread popular values. Here we find a rare harmony between the exigencies of economic growth and the desire for individual advancement. Nevertheless, some of the frictions created by socioeconomic change are being reinforced by education, the main agent of this change. Here, alienation between generations with different educational levels comes to mind, as well as the protracted lag between maturity and earning power on the part of the individual. And symptoms of an oversupply of holders of advanced degrees have appeared. But it is too early to say if this new development reflects the beginning of a reduction in differences—income and otherwise—between college graduates and their less educated contemporaries.

5. Some Effects on Life-style

Stephen B. Withey

When people talk about reasons for going to college, after mentioning economic and work benefits, they usually speak of things such as understanding the world and oneself, getting along well with people, having a chance to meet other people, and getting the chance to develop interests and a better life (Campbell & Eckerman, 1964). Many of these things are involved in "quality of life" or "life-style." There are numerous components to the concept and much discussion has occurred recently on what they are, how they relate, and the meaningfulness of this or that priority. We have referred to some of these components and will look at a few more in discussing social involvement and political leadership, health services as an example of using society's resources, behavior within the family, and some attitudes about society. These do not cover all aspects of life-style, but a look at them provides a broad-brush modal picture of the life-styles of college graduates.

ORGANIZA-TIONAL IN-VOLVEMENT There is some problem in defining "an organization" to which people belong, since there are various degrees of voluntary involvement and various meanings to membership. Nevertheless, it appears (Axelrod, 1956; Wright & Hyman, 1966) that about 60 percent of the population belongs to one or more formal groups. One can raise this figure by broadening the meaning of "formal group" or including a time span of years over which membership or association is to be recorded.

However defined, it is clear that membership is related to education. Figures vary, but most studies seem to show that membership in organizations is about half again as common among college graduates as among high school graduates. The number of organizations to which college graduates belong also increases with education, as does the proportion of those who are very active and assume positions of leadership.

Some memberships are related to occupational role and some to social status. Both are defined somewhat by educational achievement. Church membership and church attendance seem to be independent of these considerations. However, studies of regular church attendance (Argyle, 1959; Lenski, 1961) consistently find that college graduates are more likely to attend church than persons with high school education or less. The difference is greater for Protestants than for Catholics. The American Institute of Public Opinion (July 20, 1954) found that when people were asked to "claim a denomination," 83 percent of the college educated reported membership in a demonination, compared with 81 percent of the high school educated and 73 percent of those with grade school education. These *differences* are much smaller than those reported for attendance, and the *percentages* are larger than the membership rolls of the nation's churches. But the order is the same as that found for church attendance (Glock, Ringer, & Babbie, 1967).

Denominational affiliations are heavily based on inheritance rather than individual choice, but there is a clear pattern of differences among denominations and educational achievement (Glock et al., 1967). The college educated appear much more in the memberships of denominations such as Episcopalian, Congregational, and Presbyterian, somewhat less among Methodist and Lutheran, and conspicuously less among Baptist and Roman Catholic. One theory suggests that social class may relate more closely to the type of religious involvement than to the degree, and the thesis has been advanced that social class played an important part in the development of American denominations.

POLITICAL LEADERSHIP
Political organizations are usually open to all who are interested, but political leadership requires wider voter support during elections. Matthews (1954) reviewed the occupations of presidents, vice-presidents, cabinet members, senators, representatives, governors and state legislators and reported "about 90 percent of each group . . . is drawn from the top 15 percent or so of the labor force" and the upper levels of educational achievement. Keller (1963) reported that 90 percent of the political elite are college graduates, and Prewitt (1970) says that there are supporting

observations to this theme in every study of political recruitment conducted in the United States. He adds:

A man's occupation, wealth, and education affect whether he becomes a member of the politically active stratum and whether he is likely to hold political office . . . the closeness of fit between social status and political participation varies from community to community and office to office, but the pattern wherein social advantage is converted to political resource is never entirely absent (Prewitt, 1970).

In a study of 87 cities around San Francisco that is probably not too unique in its results although figures may vary regionally, Prewitt (1970) found that city councilmen present the same pattern. While the median education for the population in these cities is a high school diploma, the median education for councilmen is a college degree. In the population of these cities, 57 percent have more than a high school diploma, but 95 percent of councilmen are educated above that level. The "best educated 5 percent," those having postgraduate and advanced professional education, are not represented among these councilmen.

HEALTH People who have completed high school or college, compared with those who started but did not finish, are more accurate in their reporting of health and illness, use of medical services, available financial resources for such services, and the cost of the services they obtain (Cannell, Fisher, & Bakker, 1961). Consequently there is a little uncertainty in many of the statistics that are obtained on such matters. Nevertheless, some differences are large and clear. (Some may need minor revision in the light of recent experience with Medicare and Medicaid.)

Higher education is clearly related to greater utilization of health services. In 1962, health expenses *per family* were $409, $449, and $554, respectively, for families headed by a non-high school graduate, a high school graduate, or a person with some college; dental costs were $44, $68, and $104. For *individuals* (at the same education levels) health expenses were, respectively, $162, $187, and $202; dental costs were $13, $25, and $41 (Wilder, 1967).

These differences are not due to different costs for the same services because a family's visits to a physician increase with the level of education of the family head (Wilder, 1969). For the respective levels of education given above, the average number of visits per year were 14.2, 16.2, and 19.5. Even when only families of five or more persons were compared, similar differences were revealed: 18.2, 20.8, and 25.9 average visits, respectively.

The picture is the same for medical insurance coverage (Ahmed, 1967). Only half of the families whose head has less than nine years of schooling have complete hospital insurance coverage, in contrast to almost four-fifths of those with 13 years or more of education. With more education, a higher proportion of family heads are likely to be employed in professions or industries where group insurance contracts that cover the whole family are available.

The situation is the same in incidence of symptoms of illness and distress. Looking particularly at symptoms of psychological distress, such as headaches, dizziness, and nervousness, a definite trend of higher symptom rates occurred for the less-educated compared with the more-educated groups. The symptoms showed the greatest number of statistically significant variations with education. But only nervousness showed a counter pattern in that the less educated had lower rates for nervousness than the more educated. But the incidence of nervous breakdown was always lower for the better educated, for each sex, at all age levels (Dupuy, Engel, Devine, Scanlon, & Querec, 1970).

MARRIAGE AND CHILD REARING About the same proportion of men have never married (13 to 16 percent) whether they have a high school diploma, or a bachelor's or postgraduate degree; but among college dropouts, about twice that number have never married. Among women, the same proportion (12 percent) of holders of high school diplomas or bachelor's degrees have never married. About twice that proportion have never married among college dropouts and those who have continued into postgraduate work (Starch, 1969).

The families of college-educated women are smaller than those of mothers with less education. But families with a college-educated mother now tend to be larger than in recent decades. The relative differences are getting smaller because the size of less-educated women's families has been dropping. College women are now planning larger families because of better incomes, earlier starts raising children, and changing advantages of family living; the college educated come from a broader sector of the population, some wanting larger families (Freedman, Whelpton, & Campbell, 1959; Whelpton, Campbell, & Patterson, 1966).

In one study the ideal, the desired, and the intended parity of college women was less than that of women with a high school education or less for white non-Catholics, Catholics, and for blacks (Ryder & Westoff, 1969). The college-educated woman is apparently able to plan well her family size. Of all socioeconomic factors considered, educational attainment is the only factor closely related to the ability of groups of wives to predict their fertility (Whelpton et al., 1966).

Before the advent of the oral contraceptive "pill," college women were more likely users of contraceptives before the first pregnancy than less-educated women, who were more likely to adopt contraceptives after the first pregnancy (Freedman et al., 1959). Among college women, 68 percent reported such use, compared with 52 percent of high school graduates, 35 percent of those who attended but had not graduated from high school, and 24 percent among women with only grade school education. In the first half decade of use of the "pill," this oral contraceptive was also reported used more by college women at all ages between 20 and 45 (Westoff & Ryder, 1968).

It is interesting that level of education does not relate to the proportion of parents who mention problems, or the proportion who mention no problems, in raising their children (Gurin, Veroff, & Feld, 1960; see also Tables 34 and 35). College-educated parents are, however, somewhat less likely to say they never feel inadequate in dealing with the problems that they have. There are also differences in the kinds of problems to which they are sensitive. The less-educated parent is more often concerned about problems of physical care and provision, especially if he or she also has a low income. But the college-educated parent is more concerned about affiliative problems and his or her own tolerance of the child's behavior.

Most research literature on child rearing emphasizes socioeconomic rather than purely educational levels, but there are studies (Bayley & Schaefer, 1960; Kagan & Freeman, 1963; Rosen, 1959) that show the college educated tend to hold developmental, future-oriented, long-range views concerning their children. They prefer that their children be curious and eager to learn, cooperative, confiding in them, and that they be happy, healthy, ambitious and

TABLE 34 *Education of respondent and indices of parental adjustment (in percent)*

	Educational attainment		
Indices of parental adjustment	*Grade school*	*High school*	*College*
Report of problems in raising children:			
Mentioned problems	71	76	75
No problems	27	23	24
Not ascertained	2	1	1
TOTAL	100	100	100
N	(646)	(955)	(337)
Frequency of feelings of inadequacy:			
A lot of times; often	15	16	19
Once in a while; once or twice	22	33	40
Never	60	47	37
Not ascertained	3	4	4
TOTAL	100	100	100
N	(424)	(632)	(224)

SOURCE: Gurin, Veroff, & Feld, 1960.

independent (some of these may be in conflict), as opposed to parents with conservative, traditional views that stress neatness, cleanliness, obedience, respect, and normative behaviors. But there is a gradient and overlap between these types and some ambiguity

TABLE 35 *Education of respondent related to kinds of problems reported in raising children and sources* of inadequacy (in percent)*

	Inadequacies			Problems		
Content of problems or feelings of inadequacy	*Grade school*	*High school*	*College*	*Grade school*	*High school*	*College*
Physical care, material provisions	38	17	11	44	31	26
Child's nonfamily adjustment				21	15	19
Obedience, discipline	8	12	10	15	29	27
Parent-child affiliative relationship	16	26	36	5	8	11
Lack of tolerance for child's behavior	10	25	25			
Other	20	16	14	11	15	15
Not ascertained	8	4	4	4	2	2
TOTAL	100	100	100	100	100	100
N	(172)	(332)	(141)	(470)	(730)	(256)

* First mentioned.
SOURCE: Gurin, Veroff, & Feld, 1960.

in their implications for actual parental behavior with a child. Thus although there are differences by education on the use of control and coercion versus encouragement and disapproval, the differences by educational attainment of parents are not large.

Mastery behavior during the first three years of life is not related to parental education (Kagan & Moss, 1962), but differences do show up in achievement behavior among pre- and early teens, particularly for boys. Both boys and girls tend to do better in secondary schools when they come from college-educated families, and they tend to go to college in greater proportions. It may well be that one advantage of higher education is that parents are better equipped as teachers in the home setting when it comes to helping sons and daughters with their education.

MORALE, HAPPINESS, AND ADJUST-MENT In their classic study of problems of adjustment, Gurin, Veroff, & Feld (1960) found education a correlate of several measures. They report two important themes: people with more education seem to be more introspective about themselves and more concerned about the personal and interpersonal aspects of their lives; and they seem to have a greater sense of well-being and satisfaction (see Tables 36–40).

TABLE 36
Relationship between education and measures of general adjustment (in percent)

	Educational attainment		
Measures of general adjustment	*Grade school*	*High school*	*College*
Extent of worries:			
Never worry	15	8	10
Worry not too much	41	46	51
Worry sometimes	4	8	9
Worry a lot	31	28	23
Worry all the time	5	5	3
Not ascertained	4	5	4
TOTAL	100	100	100
Evaluation of present happiness:			
Very happy	23	39	43
Pretty happy	56	54	51
Not too happy	20	7	5
Not ascertained	1		1
TOTAL	100	100	100

SOURCE: Gurin, Veroff, & Feld, 1960.

	Educational attainment		
Marital adjustment indices	Grade school	High school	College
Evaluation of marital happiness:			
Very happy	38	46	60
Above average	16	25	22
Average	41	27	17
Not too happy	5	2	1
Not ascertained			
TOTAL	100	100	100
Frequency of feeling inadequate:			
A lot of times; often	10	13	10
Once in a while; once or twice	34	42	53
Never	53	42	33
Not ascertained	3	3	4
TOTAL	100	100	100
Report of marriage problem:			
Had problems	33	44	45
No problem	56	50	51
Inapplicable*	5	2	1
Not ascertained	6	4	3
TOTAL	100	100	100
N	(553)	(950)	(362)

TABLE 37 *Relationship between education and marital adjustment indices (in percent)*

* Refers to 50 people who evaluated their marriage as "not too happy" and therefore were not asked whether or not they ever had problems.
SOURCE: Gurin, Veroff, & Feld, 1960.

Their introspectiveness is shown in the greater prevalence of feelings of inadequacy as a parent, husband or wife, by their reports of *both* positive and negative aspects of the self, and reports of difficulty in getting things done. However, in addition to these symptoms of self-awareness and criticism, the context of evaluations of the highly educated reflects a greater awareness of the potential for gratification or frustration of emotional needs in various aspects of life. The highly educated are more likely to report interpersonal sources of present happiness, the marital relationship as a source of both marital happiness and unhappiness, interpersonal aspects of parental inadequacies, and ego-relevant sources of both job satisfaction and dissatisfaction. It appears that greater education implies a much more sensitive, aware appreciation of self and interpersonal potentials.

TABLE 38
Relationship between education and job adjustment measures among employed men (in percent)

Job adjustment measures	Educational attainment		
	Grade school	High school	College
Job satisfaction:			
Very satisfied	21	28	36
Satisfied	60	43	41
Neutral	7	6	3
Ambivalent	5	11	11
Dissatisfied	6	10	7
Not ascertained	1	2	2
TOTAL	100	100	100
N	(282)	(423)	(214)
Report of work problems:			
Had problems	21	30	37
Had no problems	79	70	63
Not ascertained			
TOTAL	100	100	100
N	(282)	(423)	(214)
Feelings of adequacy on job:			
Very good	31	28	35
Little better than average	34	41	54
Just average or not very good	34	30	8
Not ascertained	1	1	3
TOTAL	100	100	100
N	(100)	(137)	(74)

SOURCE: Gurin, Veroff, & Feld, 1960.

However, the second theme—the greater sense of well-being—implies an inbalance resolution of this evaluative sensitivity. The less-educated woman's introspectiveness seems to make her sensitive to the stressful aspects of her life. But college-level men and women seem to be more aware of positive and negative aspects of their lives and are happier in their lives, their marriages, and their jobs. They are also more optimistic about the future.

These two themes that run through the data seem to point to education as broadening one's perspective and raising the aspiration level, which leads to problems and frustrations as well as challenges and a greater awareness of life satisfactions.

It should be noted that these educational differences occur even when another important factor in social status and good living is held constant, namely income. Thus, the findings on the

TABLE 39 *Relationship between education and sources of job satisfaction among employed men (in percent)*

Sources of job satisfaction	Educational attainment		
	Grade school	High school	College
Mentioned only ego satisfactions	46	54	68
Mentioned both ego and extrinsic satisfactions	25	26	21
Mentioned only extrinsic satisfactions	19	17	8
Mentioned no reasons for liking job	5	1	
Not ascertained	5	2	3
TOTAL	100	100	100
N	(282)	(423)	(214)

SOURCE: Gurin, Veroff, & Feld, 1960.

greater satisfactions associated with higher education cannot be viewed merely as a reflection of the greater material advantages that also tend to come with higher education. But the reverse statement has some truth: high- and low-income groups at each educational level still differ in their evaluations of current happiness. Greater income is associated with greater happiness, but this finding breaks income at the median income level, so that its influence is not that of "wealth" as much as "comfort."

PREJUDICE, VIOLENCE, AND RATIONALITY Prejudice can take many forms, but religious, racial, and ethnic prejudices have been studied most. Most studies show an inverse relation between education and prejudice. Only one (Campbell, 1947, on anti-Semitism) is an exception, and the researcher now

TABLE 40 *Relationship between education and sources of dissatisfaction with the job among employed men (in percent)*

Sources of job dissatisfaction	Educational attainment		
	Grade school	High school	College
Mentioned only ego dissatisfactions	15	19	28
Mentioned both ego and extrinsic dissatisfactions	6	10	15
Mentioned only extrinsic dissatisfactions	49	45	34
Mentioned no reasons for disliking job	30	23	19
Not ascertained		3	4
TOTAL	100	100	100
N	(282)	(423)	(214)

SOURCE: Gurin, Veroff, & Feld, 1960.

(private communication on anti-black prejudice, 1970) reports that there is a difference in the impact of college experience on such issues between the pre- and post-World War II periods. He also reports significant differences by college attended, so that the picture is complex. A review and reanalysis of 26 studies by Stember (1961) finds no clear-cut relationship, but rather that previous conclusions have been a function of the type of prejudice, its timing, and how it was assessed.

Apparently, the relation of education to prejudice has varied with the political and social climate. The educated seem to be more labile than others and more responsive to changing values and beliefs. The less educated seem more bound by traditional images, established policies, and fixed forms of behavior. Stember also finds an assessment problem that has to do with the verbal terms of prejudice. When the same issues, as posed in common scales, are put in more neutral terminology, the evidence changes. The educated tend to discredit and disagree with the sharpest statements of prejudice, but less stark statements and more covert expressions gain broader support.

In the case of anti-Jewish prejudice, the positive effects of education usually are visible at each step of achievement. But reduction of prejudice against blacks is principally a function of college training. Earlier schooling generally produces little favorable change. It would appear, then, that not all increments in education are equally significant. Only a high level of education seems to exert any appreciable impact on the more deeply rooted prejudices.

It has been widely held that educated people show less prejudice simply because they usually come from the higher socioeconomic strata, where prejudice is allegedly less prevalent . . . [The data] by and large, do not support this hypothesis. More often than not, effects of education persist when socioeconomic factors are controlled. There is no conclusive evidence that those in the higher socioeconomic strata are, in fact, less prejudiced . . . [Moreover] the positive effects of education are strongest and most systematic among persons of lower status, rendering them considerably less prejudiced than even the educated of the upper status group. At higher status levels the effects of education diminish . . . [Also] on some issues the effect of socioeconomic status varies with the education of respondents. Among the least educated, those of high status show the lowest degree of prejudice. Among the most educated the reverse is true; those of low status show the least prejudice. This tendency is apparent principally in connection with discrimination against Negroes. . . .

The effects of education then, are circumscribed by subcultural factors. Only where education differentiates the individual sharply from his previous subculture does it appreciably affect his attitudes toward minorities (Stember, 1961).

The better informed are usually less prejudiced, but information alone is not a determining factor. The urbanized, too, are usually less prejudiced, but education remains visibly effective, in most cases, where degree of urbanization is controlled. Also, the educated are more likely to have contact with minority-group members, and the data show that acquaintance with blacks of respondents' own educational level reduces prejudice independently of education. But, although other factors have an influence, "the favorable effects of education per se remain evident when other possible causes are controlled" (Stember, 1961).

Summarizing his analyses, Stember finds that the educated are *less* likely to hold traditional stereotypes, less likely to favor discriminatory policies, and less likely to reject casual contacts with minority-group members. But, the educated are *more* likely to hold certain highly charged and derogatory stereotypes, more likely to favor informal discrimination in some areas of behavior, and more likely to reject intimate contacts with minority-group members.

In the area of prejudice, Stember notes that by and large, women seem more influenced by education than men, though not consistently on all issues and aspects. The difference appears principally in questions dealing with blacks. This may be in line with one of Stember's major theses that education is most effective where subcultural differences between the educated and uneducated are greatest and where homogeneity-creating forces of a political, religious, or cultural nature are minimized.

Prejudice is usually regarded as involving an irrational component, but this is rarely measured or studied systematically. It is also possible, of course, to find individuals who are irrationally "pro" some group as well as those who are irrationally "anti" in their prejudices. Schuman and Harding (1964) constructed a questionnaire that particularly focused on prejudice as a failure of rationality. Prejudice was not viewed as a kind of disease; rather persons were regarded as acting in accord with certain values—positive and negative—which may or may not have included a concern for rationality. Their questions forced respondents at one point or another to choose between adherence to the norm of rationality and adherence to other preferred values.

They report:

Education has a dramatic effect in reducing gross and inconsistent irrationality, but below the senior college level it does not greatly increase positive adherence to the norm of rationality. Extended college experience radically increases the amount of rationality, but even so, a large proportion of college graduates continue to show irrational bias with regard to ethnic groups — mainly bias in favor of minorities. This favorable bias is typically associated with a predominantly aesthetic or humanitarian value orientation (Schuman & Harding, 1964).

In a national sample of men aged 16 to 64 (Blumenthal, Kahn, & Andrews, 1971) on attitudes toward several matters related to violence, those with college experience tended to define violence more in line with the dictionary rather than include concepts, such as affront, effrontery, or challenge. For example, they were more likely to define "police beating students" as violence and less likely to think of "draft card burning" as violence. They were less supportive or tolerant of recourse to violence for *social control,* that is, high levels of force by police, than those with less education, apparently able to think of intermediary strategies before turning to this "last resort." Acceptance of violence for *social change* receives lower support generally but with little difference shown by various educational levels.

On a number of value measures — such as humanitarianism, kindness, conservatism, the relative valuation of persons and property, self-defense, and retributive justice — educational attainment had some low predictability to differing positions on these scales. For example, education made one more liberal or humanitarian, lower on retributive justice, high on kindness, or showed no relationship to rights of self-defense.

The somewhat better educated are somewhat less likely than the average to believe that violence was necessary to produce needed change fast enough. Among the educated, however, those who expressed a greater belief in equality, human dignity, and freedom were more apt to express the feeling that violence was necessary. These opinions might be interpreted as an expression of cynicism about the capacity for the social system to ameliorate social problems.

The main finding seemed to be that those with college education, though not showing consensus on separate values or on goals for societal change or control, did show more consistency, better organization, and greater rationality in values and attitudes. They "hung together" better with fewer contradictory attitudes than shown by the less educated, who often seemed to show no consistency or predictability from one attitude or value area to another.

Another small but neat piece of confirmatory evidence for consistency and rationality among information, attitudes, and behavior related to educational attainment is offered by Cannell and MacDonald (1956). They found that belief in a relationship between smoking and cancer showed little relation to acceptance of the new information and smoking. If anything, the smokers who had less than high school education were a little more likely to believe the warnings than the nonsmokers. Only those with college education showed a strong *pattern* of either belief in the hazard and cessation of smoking or scepticism coupled with continuing to smoke. The proportion who believed there were dangers to health did not vary more than 6 percent across all educational levels.

6. Mass Media Usage by the College Graduate

John P. Robinson

It can be argued that outside of schools, the mass media are the most important educational institutions in society. By now it is well understood that most individuals will spend at least three times as much of their lives in contact with the mass media as in school. Analysis of social survey data shows a distinctive pattern for college graduates in use of the media. One result of this media use is that the college educated turn out, in study after study, to be better informed about subjects such as political issues (Campbell, Converse, Miller, & Stokes, 1960), business problems (Fisher & Withey, 1951), foreign affairs (Metzner, 1949), and science and medicine (Davis, 1958). The evidence, however, is not clear to what degree education is responsible.

The basic media-use pattern can be stated briefly: the greater one's education, the greater the dependence on the printed media, and the lesser the dependence on the broadcast media. This fundamental relation tends to hold regardless of whether the aspect of media investigated is the amount of time spent with each medium, or a subjective estimate of the media from which most of the news is received (normally or during periods such as elections). Some rough idea of the magnitude of these differences can be gained by considering that in a 1965–66 national study of urban adult patterns of time use, college graduates reported 59 minutes of television viewing on an average day, versus 95 minutes for the rest of the sample (Robinson & Converse, 1966). On the other hand, college graduates reported 41 minutes on all types of reading, versus 29 minutes for the rest of the sample. This rule-of-thumb is a useful one against which to consider the discussion here, although we will note certain exceptions as the analysis becomes more complex.

Analysis is, of course, severely constrained by the types of media-usage data available from surveys of representative national samples. A thorough national inventory of the mass media habits of Americans has yet to be carried out. There have been numerous competent studies of patterns of newspaper reading (usually in single cities) or of television viewing, but no serious attempt to identify cross-media relations and what they imply. Little effort has been made to identify the consequences of various media-usage patterns in terms of gains in audience knowledge or changes in attitude, and no studies of what it means for a person to be exposed to mass media content over an extended period of time. For that reason, the analysis here is confined mainly to making as much sense as possible from the plethora of media-usage data collected by different researchers using different procedures for vastly different purposes.

Despite these less than ideal data sources, however, certain convergences in the data do emerge; and many of the differences we discuss are as predictable and stable as can be found in social-behavior data. It is likely that additional systematic research into the more dynamic aspects of media usage will reveal further differences of a similar magnitude.

PRINTED MEDIA USAGE Time spent with the newspaper is twice that spent on the other two major printed media, magazines and books (Robinson & Converse, 1966). Despite the attention drawn to the number of newspapers that have gone out of business in the last 20 years, newspaper reading is still more likely to be a daily habit of Americans than television viewing. Partly for this reason, educational differences with respect to time spent with the newspaper are not large. Nevertheless, readership studies have invariably found that college-educated persons pay far more attention to the serious content in the newspaper, such as national and international news and editorials, than to the comics, reports of crimes and accidents, and advice to the lovelorn (e.g., Robinson, 1967).

The most pronounced effects of college education can be found for readership of magazines, especially for news and analytic-commentary publications. The data in Table 41 summarizes the findings of a 1969 nationwide readership study by the Starch organization, a leading magazine-research enterprise. Not only are college-educated men and women more likely to read "highbrow" magazines like the *New Yorker* (differentials of the same

TABLE 41 *Readership of selected magazines for college graduates and the rest of the population (in percent)*

	Men		Women	
	College graduates	Rest of population	College graduates	Rest of population
Analytic commentary				
New Yorker	3	*	4	*
New York Times Magazine	10	1	11	1
National Observer	2	1	3	*
News				
Newsweek	12	3	7	2
Time	23	4	21	4
General interest				
Life	24	10	22	9
Look	17	10	16	10
Parade	19	17	21	19
Reader's Digest	34	22	37	24
TV Guide	19	18	17	21
Monthlies				
Holiday	4	1	6	1
National Geographic	20	6	19	5
Better Homes & Gardens	6	4	18	12
Men's				
Field and Stream	2	3	*	*
Mechanics Illustrated	2	2	*	*
True	4	4	2	2
Playboy	16	8	6	3
Sports Illustrated	5	2	1	1
Women's				
Modern Screen	*	*	*	1
True Story	*	*	*	3
Ladies Home Journal	4	2	17	10
Cosmopolitan	*	*	2	2
McCalls	5	3	22	22

Less than 0.5%.

SOURCE: Daniel Starch & staff, 1969.

magnitude have been found for other magazines of this genre, such as *Saturday Review* and *Harpers*) and news magazines, but also the largely pictorial *Life* and *Look*. Moreover, greater magazine reading for the college educated extends to monthlies, *Holiday, National Geographic, Playboy,* the "home" magazines, most ladies' magazines, and even to the *Reader's Digest*.

That this finding should occur is not surprising after reflection on the college graduates' greater ability to pay for a luxury item such as a magazine,[1] an expense which has very little direct economic benefit. It is instructive to see that certain other magazines are more likely to reach the noncollege segments of society—notably *Field and Stream, Mechanics Illustrated,* and *True* for men, movie, TV, and romance magazines for women. Content may thus be a stronger final determinant of magazine usage than cost. Moreover, it is necessary to keep in mind that the data in Table 41 should not be used to obscure the fact that the majority of readership for all these magazines (except the *New Yorker*) is still comprised of citizens who have not graduated from college.

Social critics may find interesting implications in Table 41 data regarding the best-educated sector of our population; for example, as high a proportion of college graduates are exposed to an average issue of *Reader's Digest* as to *Time* or *Newsweek* combined. Also, more college men read *Ladies Home Journal* and *McCalls* than the *New Yorker* or *National Observer*. And an average issue of the leading women's magazines (or *TV Guide*) reaches almost as many, if not more, college-educated women than *Time* or *Newsweek*. However, equal interest is merited in certain aspects of television viewing experiences of the college educated. Despite shorter viewing times, the college graduate still spends more time with television than with all other mass media combined. And more college graduates cite television as their major source of information about political candidates during election campaigns than all other media combined.

Less is known about the book-reading habits of Americans. The popularity of most individual titles has such a short life-span that detailed market studies, such as those of Starch for magazines, are not feasible. Data from the Starch survey do indicate that 59 percent of college graduates had purchased at least one hard-

[1] The data in Table 41 refer to persons who have either subscribed to or bought a particular issue, but not to those who may have seen a secondhand copy passed on by a neighbor or read in a doctor's office.

cover book and 61 percent a paperback in the preceding year, versus 21 and 24 percent, respectively, for the rest of the population. Time-budget data also indicate that book reading is highly stratified by education.

Data from the time-budget study suggest an interesting further differential by educational level: while readership of religious books was nearly constant across educational groups, the less educated read the Bible, and the better educated more interpretative and contemporary religious material. The relatively high proportion of do-it-yourself and nonserious fiction books also obscures educational differences in the general book-reading figures noted above. When these were eliminated from analysis in a 1957 national study of mass media habits, it was found that 24 percent of college graduates reported reading a serious nonfiction book in the previous year versus only 6 percent for the rest of the population (Robinson, 1967).

BROADCAST MEDIA

From its inception in American society, television has never been as avidly followed by the college graduate as by his less-educated fellow citizens. Despite their greater ability to afford television sets, college graduates in the early days lagged well behind high school graduates in their purchase of a set (Bogart, 1958). As television began to saturate American society (ownership was 85 percent in 1958 and has risen only 10 percent since), those who had not finished high school became the heaviest users of television; and because of their greater numbers, they have probably been responsible for some audience control of typical television fare.

This could be one of the reasons that the lower amounts of television viewing among college graduates has been a persistent finding in social science data (although such differences apparently do not persist for those over age 50). Their lower TV viewing times,[2] however, more likely arise from the fact that they have less time available for such activity. Examination of their leisure time, which is about equal in amount to that of the less educated

[2] These lower viewing times hold for viewing as a primary activity, but for secondary-activity viewing—i.e., viewing to the accompaniment of other activities—the college graduate reports more time spent. A correlative survey into the attention level of viewers found that college graduates generally report lower levels of full attention to the screen when viewing. At the same time, they are better able to retain content, if studies of the retention of advertising content is any reliable guide (Bogart, 1967).

(Robinson & Converse, 1966), shows that they are more likely to be taking adult education courses, talking with other people, or reading—the latter media activity offering the more selective variety of content that probably characterizes the information-seeking of the more idiosyncratic college graduate. College graduates' lower interest in television viewing was further reflected in this time study in that no higher proportion of college graduates mentioned some time during a typical day when they "would have liked to watch television, but did not because there were no programs worth watching at that time." There would appear to be something beyond content that accounts for the college graduate's shorter viewing times.

Among college graduates, there are consistent and unsurprising differences in preferences, compared with those of the rest of the population. When asked to name their favorite television shows, college graduates are more likely to put at the top of their list news programs, documentaries, serious drama, and programs on educational television (Steiner, 1963). Their numbers in audiences for evening movies (e.g., "Tuesday Night at the Movies") are disproportionately high and drop off significantly for almost all situation comedies and action-adventures (Simmons, 1969). And while they are no more likely than other citizens to comprise the audience for television news programs, news and documentary viewing accounts for 20 percent of their total television fare, versus only 10 percent for the rest of the population.

Before becoming sanguine about this image of the college graduate's pursuit of the factual, note the ten television programs that drew the greatest proportion of college graduates to their sets during the fall of 1968, alongside comparable data for the rest of the population (Table 42). The data come from the Simmons study (1969) of media audiences, in which over 6,000 adults kept diaries of their TV viewing over a two-week period.

The table shows that more college graduates saw an episode of "Bonanza" than a typical evening news program, and the figure is more than double that for the documentary programs "Sixty Minutes" and "First Tuesday".[3] Moreover, five of the top ten programs for college men (and four for college women) are identical to those of the rest of the population, indicating little elitism in the taste-preference patterns of the college-educated viewer.

[3] On the other hand, the overall audience for these documentaries is larger than for either *Time* or *Newsweek*.

TABLE 42 *Ten favorite television programs in terms of percentages watching in fall 1968*	*Program*	*Percent of college graduates*	*Program*	*Percent of those who did not graduate from college*

Program	*Percent of college graduates*	*Program*	*Percent of those who did not graduate from college*
	Men		
Laugh-In	24	Bonanza	23
NFL Football	24	Gunsmoke	22
Mission Impossible	23	Dean Martin	19
Monday Night Movie	19	Laugh-In	19
Smothers Brothers	19	Virginian	19
NCAA Football	19	NFL Football	19
Tuesday Night Movie	18	Red Skelton	15
Dean Martin	17	Smothers Brothers	15
Sunday Night Movie	15	Mission Impossible	14
Ironside	13	Gomer Pyle	14
	Women		
Laugh-In	24	Bonanza	24
Dean Martin	22	Family Affair	24
Family Affair	21	Laugh-In	22
Smothers Brothers	20	Mayberry RFD	21
Bonanza	19	My Three Sons	21
Ed Sullivan	19	Here's Lucy	17
Ironside	18	Dean Martin	17
Monday Night Movie	18	Julia	17
Huntley-Brinkley	17	Gomer Pyle	16
Carol Burnett	17	Beverly Hillbillies	16

SOURCE: Simmons, 1969.

Further evidence emerged when Steiner (1963) asked respondents to describe their favorite program, using a list of adjectives. As noted above, college graduates were relatively unlikely to list popular adventure programs or situation comedies. However, among those who did, higher percentages described these programs as "creative," "tasteful," or "intellectual" than in the rest of the population. In other words, the college graduate appears to perceive these programs as more sophisticated than some others might. Steiner found further that while the college graduate (in his terms, the "average non-average viewer") expressed the desire for more educational and informational material on television, this desire found little translation into behavior when an informative program was pitted against light entertainment in the television schedule. When a serious information program was on the air, 5 percent of college graduates and 4 percent of those with less education viewed it; therefore, even if college graduates existed in larger proportions, there probably would be no revolutionary demands for more sophisticated television content.

With respect to radio, we must qualify the rule stated at the beginning of this chapter. The better educated currently listen to slightly more radio, a phenomenon that appears to be the result of the influence of television. Pretelevision audience studies indicate the less educated had been more frequent radio users (Lazarsfeld, 1946). Television has had greater impact on radio than any other medium. It subsumed the function of America's most popular radio programs and apparently left demands for radio programming that would have as much appeal to the college educated as to other sectors of the population. The time study indicates that the college educated are particularly drawn to specialized radio music—classical, jazz, show tunes, and folk. And there is strong evidence that the rise of progressive or underground rock music is due to its popularity among children of the college educated, the segment also most likely to listen to more serious and complex music on their high-fidelity equipment.

Less is known about the pre-television composition of movie audiences in America, although there is little doubt that this audience is now disproportionately drawn from the ranks of the college educated.[4] It recently has been estimated that during an average month, 38 percent of college graduates attend a movie, versus 22 percent of the rest of the adult population (Starch, 1969). Movies have changed technically and artistically in the last few years, but some unusual (e.g., "Green Berets," "Love Bug") movies have been popular attractions in this audience dominated by college graduates and graduates-to-be.

Further Considerations and Elaborations of These Media-Usage Patterns Questions arise as to the context in which media-usage data characterizing the current American scene can be interpreted. Are they hopelessly idiosyncratic to our current affluent society, or can one find parallels in other societal situations? We have mentioned briefly our reasons for believing that, outside of the com-

[4] It is more stratified by age—59 percent of those aged 18–24 attend at least one movie during a month.

plexities introduced by television (mainly displacing radio drama and comedy, reading of light fiction in books and magazines, and movie attendance), the situation has not changed drastically over the last 50 years. The changes brought by increases in the percentage of the population attending college are far more significant than any changes within any of the media per se. For example, even in the earliest days of television, the college graduate appears to have been a less avid television viewer.

Moreover, impressions gained from the meager data available from other societies suggest that these patterns have cross-cultural generality as well. Time-usage data from other societies, directly comparable to that obtained in the United States survey, reveal the same educational reading differentials as found in the United States. Newspaper reading shows only minor increases with educational attainment, while college graduates read considerably more magazines and books. The shorter television viewing times of the college graduates are common in Western European societies, but interestingly do not hold up in socialist Eastern Europe. In fact, in some of these settings college graduates watch more television than their less-educated counterparts (Robinson & Converse, 1970). In these societies television content is also more along the lines of educational television in America (which is viewed here more by the college graduate than by the rest of society).

It also must be noted that our arbitrary dichotomy of the population into college graduates and nongraduates obscures the progressive increase in reading and decrease in television viewing[5] that characterize individuals with progressively greater amounts of education. To take male readership of *Life* magazine as one example, 4 percent of that quarter of the population who have had no high school exposure are readers, 8 percent of high school dropouts, 12 percent of high school graduates, 17 percent of those with some college exposure, 24 percent of college graduates, and 26 percent of those with at least some postgraduate work. Thus the relationships discussed here tend to hold across the educational spectrum.

Wilensky (1964) was one of the first sociologists to emphasize

---

[5] There is conflicting evidence on whether or not the least-educated segment of society—those who did not attend high school—watch more television than those at the next rung of formal education—the high school dropout. Part of the problem lies in the lower rates of set ownership within the least-educated segment.

the need to separate college graduates with postgraduate training from those who had none in accounting for patterns of mass media usage. He found this distinction and the quality of the college from which the person had graduated important predictors of respondents' exposure to "high-brow" media content and reticence to view "low-brow" television fare. In fact, Wilensky concluded, perhaps from inappropriate samples, that these two variables accounted for greater differences in media usage than exposure to college alone.

Wilensky also found significant differences between college graduates who gravitated into different occupations. Those who went into engineering were clearly less sophisticated users of the media than lawyers, who in turn were less likely to be consumers of high-brow fare than professors. More intriguing, however, were differences uncovered *among* respondents in the same occupation — lawyers who worked for a firm rather than on their own, engineers who worked for a company that manufactured a variety of products rather than a single product, and professors who taught in an urban rather than a church-related university. In each case the former were more sophisticated users than the latter.[6]

Research into the media habits of college graduates in the higher echelons of our society reveals that top decision makers and the business elite are particularly selective in their media habits (Robinson, 1967). Time pressures in the hectic life-styles of these busy individuals undoubtedly account for their almost total lack of contact with television.[7] Greater selectivity in magazine reading is also more apparent than is found among other college graduates, and there is substantial reading of analytic commentary magazines and news magazines (and such quality newspapers as the *New York Times* and *Wall Street Journal*). On the other hand, readership of *Look, Life,* and *Reader's Digest* is noticeably lower. However,

[6] One of the most interesting indicators of mass media usage that Wilensky employed in his study was whether, during the extremely lengthy interview, the respondent vocalized any clear hint of cultural criticism. Here the effects of college education came sharply into focus: while 76 percent of professors, 44 percent of lawyers, and 32 percent of engineers indicated such criticism, only 13 percent of general middle-class respondents (18 percent among white-collar workers and 8 percent for blue-collar workers) and 3 percent of unemployed "underdogs" did.

[7] The "Today" program appears to be one major exception, especially for decision makers in Washington. One wonders if football might not constitute a similar exception.

should relevant content appear in these less prestigious magazines (or in special reports), subordinates usually draw the attention of the elites to such material.

DETERMI-
NANTS AND
CONSE-
QUENCES OF
MEDIA USAGE

This chapter opened with the viewpoint that the media be considered the primary educational institution for adults in our society. A major theme that has emerged from studies of mass media usage is that people attend to media content that is consistent with their existing tastes. We find that the college graduate is generally more likely to use the media for educational and informational purposes. It is no accident, then, that we also find the graduate most informed about world events.

Thus there is a strong likelihood that people who are already well informed will pick up most information from the mass media, resulting in an increasing "knowledge gap" between best-informed and least-informed citizens. In the classic "Cincinnati experiment" (NORC, 1947), it was found that people who were most likely to pick up information about the United Nations during an information campaign were those who were already well informed at the outset of the campaign. Tichenor, Donohue, and Olien (1970) have provided more recent corroborative evidence of the same phenomenon on a wider variety of topics—the belief that man would reach the moon and the belief that cigarettes cause cancer. They conclude, ". . . the mass media seem to have a function similar to that of other social institutions: that of reinforcing or increasing existing inequities."

Tichenor et al. realize that not all the returns are in regarding this contention. Nevertheless, the pattern of existing empirical results points strongly in this direction. It is important, however, to realize that the "knowledge gap" does not emerge suddenly at adulthood, but begins much earlier. The current probability of college attendance for a youngster born to a father who is a college graduate is about 90 percent, but drops to one-third for anyone else. In other words, disproportionate numbers of college graduates have grown up in a home where greater value is placed on learning and greater stress on developing skills that allow one to attend and finish college with relative ease. Moreover, the college graduate has probably grown up in a neighborhood where his friends are likely to be college-bound and where teachers in school are more oriented to preparing their students for college life.

Researchers studying the impact of television on children have concluded that these forces, in addition to the child's innate orientations, combine to determine taste levels and patterns of media usage by the time the child is ten or twelve years old. Up to this point at least, the television experiences of these children are quite similar in terms of hours and programs viewed. During junior high school, however, sharp decreases appear in time devoted to television among most of those students who will eventually make their way to college. The subtle processes of reinforcement from teachers, parents, and the child's own experience combine to strengthen the college-bound student's interest in, and utilization of, the printed word. It would be rash to dismiss these factors during the child's formative years as having little influence on the media-usage patterns found among adults who have had college experience.

While college obviously results in book learning, available evidence suggests that college exposure by itself produces little, if any, effect on political knowledge. McClintock and Turner (1962) found the political knowledge of freshmen equivalent to that of seniors (given the same grade point averages). Despite the arresting nature of these findings, the implications need to be advanced with greatest caution; it may have been true a decade ago but not now. The McClintock and Turner study still seems worth replicating under today's conditions and with a proper longitudinal design.

Current data on adult attention to *news* further suggest that the postcollege period is one of "latency" for the college graduate. The 20-to-29 age group becomes enmeshed in concerns about occupation, marriage, family, and leisure life-style; it is only some 20 years later, when children are finally away from home, that one finds dramatic rises in following news events. At this juncture, it is crucial to have previously developed interests and skills to follow sophisticated accounts of world happenings. It also helps to have friends and work acquaintances with similar orientations stimulating interest and adding interpretations of what is going on, for it is also found that the college graduate is more likely to become involved in discussions of the same serious news content put forth by the media.

The preceding discussion has generally emphasized the necessity of examining several aspects of the influence of education on media usage, and the timing of impact within stages of the lifespan. Attempts to isolate college experience per se, as a key determinant of the media-usage patterns noted in preceding sections, have not yet been successful. Persons who attend college deviate from their noncollege peers in a number of ways before they attend their first lecture. Once out of college, the graduate uses the media to become even more knowledgeable about his wider environment. It is not implausible that the college experience, by inculcating an appreciation of wider experiences and interests and feelings of responsibility and rational management, contributes substantially to the student's motivation to keep abreast of world happenings through the mass media once he has left the confines of the campus.

SUMMARY AND IMPLICATIONS FOR THE FUTURE   In reviewing existing evidence on the mass media habits of college graduates, we find many facets that distinguish this group from the rest of the audience for mass communications. The far greater reliance on magazines and books for sophisticated and analytical content, unavailable from television, definitely sets college graduates apart from the rest of the population. Moreover, such tendencies become even more pronounced with greater levels of education and employment in society's more responsible occupations.

At the same time, one should not overemphasize such differences since there certainly is considerable similarity in many facets of media usage. The daily contact of college graduates with the newspaper and radio is similar in duration to the rest of the population's, but college graduates are somewhat different in what they pay attention to. And while they spend far less time viewing television, the time is still greater than on all other mass media combined—as is true for the influence they attribute to the various media in keeping them informed. Nor are the programs viewed in greatest numbers particularly marked by uniqueness or excellence. If society did not provide college graduates means for alternative use of their leisure time, there is some reason to believe they could as easily center far more of their free time on current fare on television.

An important issue has been raised concerning the media's role in increasing the "knowledge gap" between the more- and less-educated segments in society. If the media in their current state foster greater differentiation in society, then prospective media developments promise only to accentuate such a trend.

The rise of specialty magazines is a phenomenon already well under way in the last decade. The only magazines[8] that have experienced growths in circulation notably in excess of the 88 percent increase in college graduates during the 1960s were those with well under the one million circulation mass market—the *New Republic,* the *National Review,* and the *Saturday Review.* The news magazines have almost managed to keep pace proportionally with the increase in college graduates, but the magnitude of increase for *Life* and *Look* (and perhaps *Ladies Home Journal, Reader's Digest,* and *Better Homes and Gardens*) is only on the order of the growth of the general population. And the convergent pattern of magazine reading among today's 18- to 24-year-old segment of the audience further reinforces the view that the current market for all but the small-market specialized magazines is likely to be constant for some time to come.

There is some question, circulation growth aside, whether large-subscription national magazines can survive the competition with television for the advertising dollar, although the recent ban on TV cigarette advertising could significantly help magazine revenues. If the national magazines were to lose this battle, as some have, the magazine market would become solely a fragmented one, with the attendant likelihood of accentuating the "knowledge gap."

Given such a scenario, television could take the role of the major national medium. Yet the most exciting innovations in television technology are similarly designed to cater to more fragmented audiences—CATV or cable television promises to allow viewers an almost unlimited choice of television programs, and EVR (videorecorders) gives viewers the potential of playing back portions of favorite programs or renting specially made cassettes with an almost unlimited variety of content. The success of either or both innovations would indicate that we should expect the breakup of mass audiences, at least at the magnitudes that we now know them, into more privatized audiences whose media experiences mainly serve to further develop individual differences that already exist.

On the other hand, there is evidence to suggest that such trends will be a long time coming, if they are on the horizon at all. The example of auditory media may be taken as instructive, since they suggest that most individuals in society prefer "live" programming

---

[8] One major exception to this observation was the magazine that had a phenomenal fivefold expansion in this period, *Playboy. National Geographic,* with almost a threefold increase, constitutes a further exception.

to continually making decisions about what to listen to. Despite the wide diffusion of phonographs and tape recorders, the time-use study still found Americans spending almost ten times more time listening to the radio than to records or tapes.

One is on perilous ground, however, generalizing from the situation in the sixties to 1990, when the proportion of college graduates could easily double, with the majority of the population having been exposed to at least some college training. It is this segment of society, we suggest, that is most likely to appreciate the variety that these new techniques can deliver. The degree to which current college training can inculcate abilities to utilize this new technology may very well determine the pace of development of these new media forms and the impact that they might have.

7. Political Behavior

Elizabeth Keogh Taylor and Arthur C. Wolfe

In the earliest days of this country's existence as an independent nation, a literate and informed mass public was thought vital to the survival of democratic government. In effect, a proposal was advanced that a relationship exists between the level of education of the citizenry and the quality of political life. The level of education reached by the average American citizen has measurably increased since the American experiment in democracy was initiated. However, the demands on the quality of political life have increased concomitantly. This chapter addresses the question of how a college education is related to the political perspectives and actions of American citizens, and what trends in these relationships may be found from the past quarter century in national political surveys.

For over 20 years, the Survey Research Center, University of Michigan, has collected data on the political attitudes and behavior, as well as the demographic characteristics, of national samples of adults of voting age. This chapter examines Survey Research Center data collected in each presidential election year from 1948 to 1968, as well as from the congressional election of 1966, and information obtained by the National Opinion Research Center in 1944. (Some variables were, of course, not included every year.)

This chapter focuses on three educational groups: college graduates, those who attended college but did not graduate, and those with no college experience. In the eight samples, the percent of college graduates changes from 6 to 13 percent, while the percent of nongraduate attenders ranges from 8 to 14 percent. An analysis of the 27 percent of the 1968 sample who had some college experience shows that 25 percent had attended "quality" schools and 75 percent had attended lower-rated institutions. Some 55 percent of the attenders of less prestigious colleges had not received a bachelor's degree, while only 33 percent of the attenders of the "quality" institutions failed to attain a degree.[1] Thus proportionately more people from prestigious institutions are in the "college graduate" category rather than in the "some college" category, and proportionately more people from the lower-rated colleges are in the "some college" category (Head, 1970).

PARTY PREFERENCE College graduates are much more likely to consider themselves affiliated (in identification, not necessarily in voting habits) with the Republican party than persons who never attended college. In each year, except 1964, considerably more graduates considered themselves Republicans than considered themselves Democrats. Throughout this period (1948–1968), only one-half to two-thirds as many nonattenders considered themselves Republicans as considered themselves Democrats. And, as shown in Table 43, nongraduate attenders tend to fall between these two groups, with a slight tendency to prefer the Democrats. Level of education has one of the strongest relationships to party affiliation of any background factor in the American system of broad-based, heterogeneous political parties.

Table 43 also indicates that there is a slight, but inconsistent, tendency for college graduates to be more independent than nonattenders, but nongraduate attenders did not, in recent elections, fall between the other two groups. There seems to be a general increase in independence over the 1944 to 1968 period among both college attenders and nonattenders, which is particularly notice-

---

[1] Colleges were ranked on a seven-point scale based on ratings of the American Association of University Professors. These ratings are based on faculty salaries and average test scores of students. The top four categories made up the "quality" stratum. It should be noted that many of the "non-quality" schools were not four-year institutions.

TABLE 43 *Comparison of party affiliation by education, 1944–1968 (in percent)*

Educational attainment	1944			1952			1956			
	Dem.	Ind.	Rep.	Dem.	Ind.	Rep.	Dem.	Ind.	Rep.	Dem.
College graduate	27	36	35	24	36	40	36	22	42	33
Some college	35	28	35	42	22	36	38	28	34	33
No college	41	28	28	50	21	26	45	23	27	48
TOTAL SAMPLE	39	29	29	47	22	27	44	23	29	45

SOURCES: 1944 national election study, National Opinion Research Center; 1948, 1952, 1956, 1960, 1964, 1966, and 1968 national election studies, Survey Research Center, The University of Michigan. (Since the data in all tables following in this chapter are from these studies, the source is not repeated hereafter.)

able among college attenders in 1968. Converse (1969) has demonstrated that there are about twice as many independents among young people aged 21 to 24 as among those over 70. With young people making up an increasing proportion of both the total electorate and the college-educated portion of the electorate, this rise in independence may be expected to continue for some time.

VOTER TURN-OUT People who have gone to college tend to exercise their right to vote, in both primary and general elections, considerably more often than those with no college experience. The proportion of people who reported voting in each presidential election since 1936, and the congressional election of 1966, is shown in Table 44. Except for the congressional election year, turnout by college graduates has been around 90 percent. In general, the turnout of nongraduate attenders has been slightly below that of the graduates and well above that of the nonattenders. In spite of the gradual increase in average educational attainment over the 34-year period, there does not seem to be any consistent trend altering electoral participation either among college attenders or the population as a whole.

The overall pattern of turnout by party and educational level between 1952 and 1968 indicates that, in general, for each educational level, Republicans are more likely to vote than Democrats, who in turn are more likely to vote than Independents. Within each group of party adherents (and for Independents as well), those with college degrees are more likely to vote than college attenders without degrees, who in turn are more likely to vote than those who have not been to college.

VOTING CHOICE As would be expected from the party-affiliation data, college graduates are much less likely than those with no college experience

1960			1964			1966			1968	
Ind.	*Rep.*	*Dem.*	*Ind.*	*Rep.*	*Dem.*	*Ind.*	*Rep.*	*Dem.*	*Ind.*	*Rep.*
26	38	38	24	37	33	27	40	27	30	35
20	46	39	30	30	39	32	29	29	43	28
23	25	56	21	22	49	28	22	51	25	22
23	29	52	23	25	46	28	25	45	29	24

TABLE 44 Respondents reporting voting in fall elections, 1936–1968* (number and percent)	Educational attainment	1936†	1940†	1944	1948	1952
	College graduate	87% (245)	89% (267)	90% (223)		93% (114)
	Some college	90% (248)	87% (262)	86% (224)	79%‡ (100)	87% (148)
	No college	81% (1,657)	82% (1,828)	80% (1,576)	61% (558)	71% (1,528)
	TOTAL SAMPLE	83% (2,158)	83% (2,365)	82% (2,027)	64% (662)	73% (1,899)

*For each education category, the numbers (N's) in parentheses are the cases in each cell on which the percentages are based. N's for the total samples include those cases for which educational level was not ascertained. For 1960, 1964, and 1968 the N's are weighted. The total unweighted N's in those years were 1,107, 1,684 and 1,488, respectively.

†From 1944 data.

‡Includes college graduates.

SOURCE: See Table 43.

to vote for Democratic presidential candidates. In none of the nine presidential elections did as many as half of the college graduates report voting for the Democratic nominee. The figures are shown in Table 45. Surprisingly, given the more Democratic identifications of the nongraduate attenders, they do not appear in general any more likely to vote Democratic than do the graduates.

Turning to congressional voting, there are similar differences among the three educational groups, but all three groups show a greater tendency to vote Democratic for congressman than for president. Only in the Democratic landslide of 1964 did the Democratic presidential candidate draw more votes from each group than did the Democratic congressional candidates. In general, a greater deviation from party identification tends to take place in

TABLE 45 *Democratic presidential vote of those voting, 1936–1968 (in percent)*

Educational attainment	1936*	1940*	1944	1948	1952	1956	1960	1964	1968
College graduate	49	42	42		29	31	38	49	35
Some college	64	48	41	23†	24	31	33	58	32
No college	67	61	55	59	45	43	53	72	44
TOTAL SAMPLE	64	57	51	53	42	40	49	67	40

* From 1944 data.
† Includes college graduates.
SOURCE: See Table 43.

1956	1960	1964	1966	1968
89%	93%	88%	81%	89%
(141)	(186)	(479)	(122)	(377)
91%	88%	89%	70%	80%
(189)	(216)	(522)	(177)	(409)
69%	76%	75%	59%	72%
(1,424)	(1,420)	(3,262)	(983)	(1,973)
73%	79%	78%	62%	76%
(1,762)	(1,827)	(4,288)	(1,288)	(2,762)

presidential voting than in congressional voting, and these deviations have tended to be in a Republican direction during the 1952 to 1968 period.

A comparison of those voters who identified with one of the major parties but voted for the other gives an indication of the strength of party allegiance at the critical point of balloting. Table 46 shows that, except for 1964 and 1966, Democrats were quite a bit more likely than Republicans to vote for the other party, especially among college attenders not graduating. The 1964 figures reflect the turning away of many Republicans from Goldwater, and it is interesting to note that, among both noncollege voters and those with some college experience, the crossover by Democrats to the Republican presidential candidate was lower than for any other presidential election year, while the crossover by Republicans to the Democratic candidate was three times greater than it was in any of the other years. However, among college graduates, although almost one in five of the Republicans voted for the Democratic candidate in 1964, an even larger proportion of Democratic graduates voted for the Republican candidate that year.

Although the 1966 election results are often interpreted as a repudiation of the Johnson administration, it is interesting to note that in the congressional vote there were more Republican identifiers who crossed to a Democrat than Democratic identifiers who crossed to a Republican in that year. This was particularly true

TABLE 46 *Comparison of Democratic party identifiers who voted for the Republican candidate for president (Congress in 1966), and Republican party identifiers who voted for the Democratic candidate, 1944–1968 (in percent)*

Educational attainment	1944		1952		1956	
	$D \rightarrow R$	$R \rightarrow D$	$D \rightarrow R$	$R \rightarrow D$	$D \rightarrow R$	$R \rightarrow D$
College graduate	23	5	48	5	25	2
Some college	20	4	50	2	39	3
No college	13	9	24	4	24	4
TOTAL SAMPLE	15	8	27	4	25	4

SOURCE: See Table 43.

among college graduates. Of course it is also true that to a large extent congressional elections are decided on local issues and are hazardously regarded as judgments of national administrations.

In general the data on crossover indicate that while Republicans at all educational levels are less likely than Democrats to vote for the other party, Republicans who have attended college are less likely to vote for the Democrats than Republicans who have not been to college. Among Democrats, those with no college experience are less likely to vote Republican than those who have been to college. This supports the important role of status cross-pressures in affecting actual partisan behavior contrary to normal partisan predisposition.

POLITICAL INFORMATION AND IDEOLOGY The expectation that college attenders would have more information than nonattenders is confirmed by the survey data. In the election studies from 1960 to 1968, respondents were asked which party had the majority in Congress both before and after the election. In each year the highest proportion of correct answers was given by college graduates (81 percent average) followed by the non-graduate attenders (74 percent average) while those with no college were least likely to name the Democrats (average 51 percent). In general, proportionately more college graduates know the name of at least one of their district's congressional candidates than do those with some college, who in turn are more likely than those with no college to name a candidate. In 1960 respondents were asked John F. Kennedy's religion, and in 1964 questions were asked about Barry Goldwater's home state and whether Communist China was a member of the United Nations. For these three questions, college graduates also were most likely to answer correctly, while people with no college experience were the least likely.

1960		1964		1966		1968	
$D \to R$	$R \to D$	$D \to R$	$R \to D$	$D \to R$	$R \to D$	$D \to R$	$R \to D$
17	3	24	19	13	20	17	10
24	5	10	18	18	19	26	4
19	8	9	31	13	16	17	7
19	7	11	27	13	18	18	7

However, more than half of the nonattenders answered the questions correctly; for example, over 90 percent knew that Kennedy was a Roman Catholic. Thus we are hardly speaking of informed versus uninformed people, but it is clear that with increasing amounts of formal education, the likelihood of acquiring a storehouse of factual information about political matters also increases.

People who have been to college seem to view the two major political parties differently than those who have not been. Respondents were asked about general differences between the two major parties and whether one party was more conservative than the other. Those who had not attended college were most likely, and college graduates least likely, to view neither party as more conservative than the other. People who had attended college but received no degree consistently fell between the two groups on this question. Similarly, persons with college degrees were more likely than nonattenders to say that other important differences existed between the parties. There are, however, fluctuating and inconsistent differences between college graduates and nongraduate attenders in this regard.

One would expect the college educated to be more articulate concerning differences between the parties and, therefore, to mention more frequently differences with issue or ideological content. The data conform to this expectation. College graduates are more likely than those with some college experience, but no degree, to mention ideological differences between the two parties; and those with some college are more likely to mention these differences than people without any college. Over 70 percent of the graduates (89 percent in 1966) who said there were important party differences mentioned ideological differences, compared to about two-thirds of the college attenders without degrees, and less than one-half of those with no college experience. These figures indicate that, in general, those with some college tend to be more like graduates than those with no college experience in terms of perception of issues separating the two parties.

POLITICAL INVOLVEMENT AND ACTIVITY
Underlying the individual's decisions with regard to participation in political activity are his general attitudes on involvement in the political system. As would be expected from the earlier data on turnout, college attenders show consistently higher *interest* in political campaigns, and they *care* more about electoral outcomes than nonattenders (Table 47). College graduates show generally higher levels of concern than do nongraduate attenders, although these differences are not so great as in the comparison with non-attenders. By no means, however, are all persons with college experience highly interested in political events. Among all groups, involvement tends to fluctuate relative to the degree of excitement generated by a national presidential campaign. Nevertheless, it is clear that a strong association exists between such interest and time spent in college.

Similar trends exist for various kinds of political participation. In general, graduates are more likely than college attenders without degrees—who are more likely than those with no college experience—to have tried to influence the vote of others (Table 48), to have written to a public official (Table 49), to have given money for political campaigns (Table 50), or to have worked for a party or a candidate (Table 51). They are also more likely to be contacted by a party representative before an election (Table 52).

POLITICAL EFFICACY
People's feelings about their effectiveness in public and political affairs have been measured using a four-item scale developed by Douvan and Walker (1956). This sense of political efficacy has been found highly related to levels of formal education, not only in this country but in other countries as well (Converse, forth-

TABLE 47
Respondents high on political interest and concern, 1952-1968 (in percent)

Educational attainment	1952	1956	1960	1964	1966	1968
College graduate	68	36	53	50	49	49
Some college	62	37	47	47	39	43
No college	30	25	30	30	25	30
TOTAL SAMPLE	33	27	34	34	29	35

SOURCE: See Table 43.

TABLE 48	Educational attainment	1952	1956	1960	1964	1966	1968
	College graduate	47	41	44	51	41	47
	Some college	43	42	44	38	38	41
	No college	24	25	31	24	17	28
	TOTAL SAMPLE	28	28	36	28	22	32

TABLE 48 *Respondents who tried to influence the vote of others, 1952–1968 (in percent)*

SOURCE: See Table 43.

TABLE 49	Educational attainment	1964	1968
	College graduate	46	47
	Some college	24	30
	No college	12	13
	TOTAL SAMPLE	17	20

TABLE 49 *Respondents who had ever written to a public official, 1964 and 1968 (in percent)*

SOURCE: See Table 43.

TABLE 50	Educational attainment	1952	1956	1960	1964	1966	1968
	College graduate	17	22	26	26	17	21
	Some college	12	14	13	19	15	11
	No college	3	8	9	7	6	6
	TOTAL SAMPLE	4	10	12	11	8	9

TABLE 50 *Respondents giving money for political campaign, 1952–1968 (in percent)*

SOURCE: See Table 43.

TABLE 51	Educational attainment	1952	1956	1960	1964	1968
	College graduate	7	11	13	17	10
	Some college	9	4	5	8	8
	No college	2	2	5	3	5
	TOTAL SAMPLE	3	3	6	5	6

TABLE 51 *Respondents who worked for a party or candidate, 1952–1968 (in percent)*

SOURCE: See Table 43.

TABLE 52
*Respondents
reporting
contact by
party
representatives
before the fall
election,
1952–1968
(in percent)*

Educational attainment	1952	1956	1960	1964	1966	1968
College graduate	19	22	34	48	35	38
Some college	14	25	32	34	30	31
No college	12	16	19	23	23	22
TOTAL SAMPLE	12	17	22	27	25	25

SOURCE: See Table 43.

coming). It is clear from the data in Table 53 that the more formal education a person has, the more likely he will see himself as having some influence on the "system." College graduates in general are two to three times as likely to score high on this measure as those with no college experience.

If, for each educational level, we compare the proportion of those who score high on political efficacy and the proportion of those who believe elections help a good deal in conveying the electorate's opinions to the government, it is evident that at all levels more respondents believed that elections helped a good deal than scored high on political efficacy. But the difference for college graduates was rather small (3 percent in 1964, 11 percent in 1968); for attenders without degrees it was a bit larger (13 percent in 1968, 23 percent in 1966); and for those with no college, the gap was largest (35 percent in 1968, 42 percent in 1964). We might conclude, then, that there is a strong belief in all segments of the population, particularly among those who show the highest degree of alienation from the political process (as measured by the political efficacy index), that the democratic process "works" because the people's wishes can be meaningfully expressed at the ballot box.

**PERSONAL
COMPETENCE** Political efficacy, as measured by the four-item scale, is strongly related to a more generic concept, the sense of *personal* competence in one's everyday life. The Coleman report on racial segregation in school found a child's sense of personal competence the best predictor of his performance in school (Converse, forthcoming).

TABLE 53
*Respondents
high on
political efficacy
index,
1952–1968
(in percent)*

Educational attainment	1952	1956	1960	1964	1966	1968
College graduate	71	77	66	66	70	59
Some college	47	74	62	53	53	46
No college	22	33	36	25	22	25
TOTAL SAMPLE	27	41	42	33	31	32

SOURCE: See Table 43.

Educational attainment	1956	1960	1964	1968
College graduate	48	65	63	51
Some college	47	58	46	47
No college	51	43	45	36
TOTAL SAMPLE	50	47	47	40

SOURCE: See Table 43.

Not unexpectedly, a similar pattern of relationship between higher educational attainment and feelings of personal efficacy is found: the more formal schooling one has, the greater the likelihood of scoring high on this measure. Tables 54 and 55 give the results, by education, for 1956 to 1968, of two of the items used in the scale, thus offering examples of both the item content and the distribution of respondents on such questions.

Competence in everyday life is not an independent or totally personal achievement. One has to work with and through others; and it is interesting to notice that college graduates, more frequently than those of progressively less educational achievement, report that they believe that most of the time people try to be helpful (Table 56). Theirs is not an uncooperative world, and apparently there is some association between education level and faith in one's fellow man.

VALUES AND ISSUES

In addition to party preference and party image, political orientation is usually molded around current issues related to political policy. Do those who have received a college degree think differently from those who did not complete a degree or from the rest of the population, on matters such as social welfare policies, civil rights, protest activities, federal aid, and the war in Vietnam?

Domestic Issues

It has been demonstrated earlier that college attenders are more likely to prefer the Republican party and to vote for Republican candidates than are people without college experience. Thus it is

Educational attainment	1956	1960	1964	1968
College graduate	83	84	77	69
Some college	80	70	71	59
No college	52	55	57	44
TOTAL SAMPLE	57	60	61	50

SOURCE: See Table 43.

TABLE 56
Respondents
who believe
that, most of
the time, people
try to be
helpful, 1964–
1968 (in
percent)

Educational attainment	1964	1966	1968
College graduate	68	71	84
Some college	60	63	62
No college	51	48	55
TOTAL SAMPLE	54	52	60

SOURCE: See Table 43.

not surprising to find that college attenders have tended to hold more conservative attitudes on a number of domestic issues concerning the proper role of the federal government. For example, in 1956 only 37 percent of college attenders, compared to 67 percent of the nonattenders, favored federal government activity for lower-cost medical care. By 1968, 48 percent of college attenders favored such activity, while the percent of nonattenders who favored government medical assistance stayed at 67 percent.

Similar but slightly smaller differences are found on the question of governmental responsibility to "see that every person has a job and a good standard of living." College attenders are also more likely to believe that the federal government is getting too powerful. In general college graduates hold somewhat more conservative views on these questions than do nongraduate college attenders, but the differences between the two college groups are not nearly so great as the differences between those with some college experience and those with no college experience. Crossing this status line between no college and some college is clearly associated with more conservative views on social welfare issues.

In regard to civil rights issues, respondents' attitudes toward the federal government's role in school integration have been assessed since 1956; and since 1964, other questions falling under the general heading of civil rights issues have been asked. There is no consistent pattern by educational level in respondents' attitudes toward the federal government's responsibility for school integration. While attitudes toward a governmental role in this area became progressively more favorable from 1956–1966 at all educational levels, in 1968 they declined rather significantly for each of the educational categories to more or less what they had been in 1956. The pattern of responses to the question "Have civil rights leaders been pushing too fast?" also shows no consistency by educational level.

General attitudes toward desegregation, however, show clear

differences by educational level, with the highest proportion favoring desegregation among college graduates, and the lowest proportion among those with no college experience. In 1964, 32 percent of the general population and 49 percent of college graduates favored desegregation; in 1968, these figures had increased to 37 percent and 61 percent, respectively. Data on attitudes toward open housing also show consistent distinctions between educational levels; and to a lesser extent, some differences over a period of time by educational levels. College graduates are more likely than attenders without degrees, who in turn are more likely than those with no college, to favor open housing for blacks.

The data on changes during the college years stressed the socialization of students to the issues of the time. This interpretation is applicable to the attitudes of college graduates on an issue such as open housing and points to the need to analyze the positions of college graduates by the decade of their college experience. Questions on open housing were included in a study of racial attitudes in 15 American cities (Campbell & Schuman, 1968). Analysis of the findings showed that

. . . years of formal education exert an influence on racial perceptions and attitudes but it is not a simple cumulative effect and it is much stronger among younger people than among older people. . . .

Among people over 40 years of age, those with higher levels of education are no more or less likely to support an open housing law . . . than people of lower educational attainment. The picture is quite different among people age 20 through 39. Here we see that the attitudes expressed by young people whose formal education has not gone beyond high school do not differ from older people of similar educational level. But those who have gone on to college differ substantially both from less-educated people of their own generation and from college-educated people of the older generation. . . .

The general pattern of these two figures recurs when we plot the answers to a wide variety of questions regarding perceptions, attitudes, and opinions (Campbell & Schuman, 1968, p. 35).

The exemplary position of the college educated on general desegregation and open housing is tarnished by their position on school integration. As Stember (1961) points out, this may be an issue that brings values "close to home" and evidences the covert and less obvious prejudices of the more educated, especially those who are old enough to be parents.

In the early 1960s, demonstrations, marches, sit-ins, and acts of civil disobedience were pretty well restricted to black civil rights activists and their few white supporters. By the mid-1960s the antiwar forces (mainly white) had also turned to demonstrations, and by the late 1960s college students in large numbers entered the ranks. There are no trend data on attitudes toward protest activities, and, if there were, they might be misleading since the protesters and the issues have changed.

In 1968, however, three questions about protest activities were asked. The answers showed that college graduates were much more likely to approve of protest marches and civil disobedience than either of the other educational groups, and those with some college were more likely than those with no college experience to approve of protest activities. At each educational level, however, obstructive activities received less approval than civil disobedience and quite a bit less approval than authorized protest marches. Only 10 percent of college graduates, 7 percent of those with some college but no degree, and 8 percent of those with no college experience gave their approval to sit-ins and similar kinds of obstructive activities.

On the 1968 question of urban unrest, people with no college experience were the most likely (23 percent of this group) of the three educational groups to approve the use of *all available force* to maintain law and order. Those with some college were a little less likely than those with no college experience, but more likely than graduates, to approve the use of all available force. On this item and the three questions on protest activities, those with some college experience seem to resemble those with no college experience much more than they resemble graduates. An alternative way to handle urban unrest—trying to get at the problems of poverty and unemployment in the cities—was more popularly supported at all three educational levels. Approximately one-third of the respondents at each educational level favored an all-out problem-solving approach. The rest proposed some mix of working on causes and use of limited enforcement.

Position on International Involvement

The college-educated sector of the public has consistently been better informed on foreign policy and international conditions, more trusting and optimistic about international relations, less apprehensive on the prospects of war, supportive of the United Nations and other peace-keeping organizations and arrangements (Scott & Withey, 1958; Survey Research Center, 1947, 1952), and more confident of military defense capability (Withey, 1954). In late 1945 when the public split on support of the new United Nations versus strong United States defenses, the college educated were almost 3 to 1 in favor of reliance on the United Nations (Scott & Withey, 1958, p. 118).

In spite of the fact that questions have differed and the level and type of this country's involvement in other parts of the world have varied tremendously over the past 26 years, college graduates have always been at least as likely, and usually quite a bit more likely, to favor international involvement than those with some college but no degree. The latter have always been more likely than those with no college experience to favor our international involvements. Whether the question has to do with foreign aid, military intervention in other parts of the world, or membership in a world organization, this relationship holds.

Respondents' beliefs as to the party best able to prevent a large-scale war have been fairly consistent. With the exception of 1964, respondents at each educational level indicate they think that the Republicans are more likely to prevent a war than the Democrats. As would be expected, college attenders, even more than the non-attenders, tend to see the Republicans as the party best able to keep the peace.

Data on attitudes toward the Vietnam war (and the Korean war in 1952) tend to support the contention that college attenders in general, and graduates in particular, have been more supportive, or "hawkish," than the rest of the population. College graduates were less likely than attenders with no degree—who were less likely than those with no college experience—to believe intervention in Vietnam or Korea a mistake. By 1968, people who had been to college were more likely than they had been previously to classify intervention in Vietnam as an error, but they were still less likely than the rest of the population to do so.

A recent detailed analysis of these data (Converse & Schuman, 1970) indicate that the locus of support for the war among the college educated is generally found among the alumni of the smaller and less prestigious institutions. It is noted:

Since this group is numerically the largest in the college-educated population, its views explain why national survey data show people of college background giving relatively strong support to the war (Converse & Schuman, 1970, p. 23).

The authors go on to say:

. . . these findings suggest rather clearly that feeling against the war has consisted up to now of two currents that are widely separated from each other. One current is made up of a tiny fraction of the population, but one that is highly educated, articulate and visible [alumni of the more prestigious institutions]. The other group [those with no college experience] tends to be less educated than the national average and is much less politically visible, although it is far larger than the set of vocal critics — perhaps by a factor of 10 or more (Converse & Schuman, 1970, p. 24).

Thus one is brought, full cycle, back to the question of the meaning of the college experience along with its continued translation into the circumstances of adult life. The type of institution seems, as in this topical area, to make a significant difference; but on other topics the type or rating of one's college seems irrelevant or the picture is muddled. For certain alumni, the course of life seems heavily influenced by the uniqueness of the institution they attended; for others it was their individual experience. For most the major impact is in having had the college experience at all and entering adult life by that bridge, instead of by others, to the occupations, resources, roles, interests, perspectives, and opportunities of the college graduate.

8. Summary and Conclusions

Stephen B. Withey

Colleges and universities in the United States have grown so fast that they have tripled in number in the last three decades. Many have also grown in size; some have more students than were in all colleges and universities before the turn of the century. The pattern of higher education has shifted rapidly from classical training in liberal arts and the humanities and preparation for the top professions, such as medicine and law, to include science and engineering; and more recently to include training in vocations, services, management, new fields of specialization, and technologies. Community, commuter, and junior colleges are examples of the growing variety of higher education institutions.

Thus, when one examines the impact of higher education he might well expect it to vary over the years to the same extent as the meaning of "college" has changed. But the situation is further complicated by the growth of the proportion of young people going to college, as well as by the increase in numbers. This increased variety of students means that colleges now try to serve people with goals, expectations, skills, abilities, and backgrounds different from those of students of previous decades.

There is now a complicated process of matching students with various resources, abilities, values, and aspirations to a variety of colleges, disciplines, curricula, educational styles, residence arrangements, and institutional orientations. For a large proportion of students who drop out, and probably for some of those who graduate, the match does not seem to work as well as it should.

Some would say that the impact of higher education should be assessed among that quarter of students who go to the "quality schools." Others would push for varied criteria, looking for and encouraging disparate consequences of the college experience.

All this variety in institutions, in shifts over time, in students, and educational purposes makes judgement of impact a complicated matter.

It is clear that the components of socioeconomic status—parents' income, occupation, and education—contribute to the likelihood of offspring attending college, as does a student's ability and interest in extended education. The influence and encouragement of parents, teachers, and the student's peers also contribute to college aspirations, as do the changing labor market and conditions of economic opportunity.

Although it is not true of all areas, it is broadly true that every year of higher education results in added impact and benefit. Those who do not complete requirements for the college degree sometimes appear more like high school graduates and sometimes more like those who have completed four years of college. But very frequently, they fall in between the diploma- and degree-achieving students. One discrepant characteristic is that nongraduates are less likely to get married than their peers in either the high school or college graduate categories.

It is also common to find that impact cumulates over generations. Sons and daughters of parents who have gone to college show attitudes, behaviors, and achievements that reflect college impact more than their fellow students who are the first generation in their family to go to college. Sons and daughters of college-trained parents have, in many ways, been trained in the values of college all their lives. Students who go to college when their parents did not have a generation gap to cope with since their lives, life-styles, and values tend to show significant changes.

There is also a widening knowledge gap between young people who graduate from college and those who do not. College graduates not only acquire new knowledge, skills, and interests; they also change in their behavior toward information. They use the printed media more—newspapers, magazines, and books—know more about what is happening in the world and how society works, and extend their attention and interests, usually, to include broader topics and international events and concerns.

Although the picture is not clear, there is evidence that particular institutions and specific curricula attract different kinds of students; and some of these differences in interests, values, and goals are further accentuated during the college experience. This impact is, of course, greater for some students than for others and depends on the goals and methods adopted by a college and what it chooses to emphasize in its "local climate." It is, however, also apparent that there is a general impact of college education across most institutions and most students. Students who start from a low socioeconomic base appear to change in the same areas, and in the same direction, as their more privileged peers.

The college experience appears more likely than not to make students more open-minded and liberal, less concerned with material possessions, more concerned with aesthetic and cultured values, more relativistic and less moralistic, but more integrated, rational, and consistent. Students tend to lessen in their adherence to traditional values and traditional behaviors. They become less authoritarian although this may be related to the social climate at the time of their education. They become more aware of themselves and of interpersonal relationships and show a greater readiness to express their emotions. These students also show lessening interest in job security and growing interest in the meaningful, interesting, and challenging aspects of an occupation.

But this, of course, is not true for all. Some institutions and some students show different patterns. Vocationally oriented students seem to show these changes less than others, and this same pattern is revealed in comparisons of students in engineering, business administration, or natural sciences with those in social sciences or the humanities.

The years of higher education are a period of delayed commitment and a moratorium during which most students are encouraged to examine issues, to reconsider their own standards, values, and identities, and to lay plans for their own role in society. It is a time of change and one in which all students participate to a certain extent. There is no doubt that, whatever the impact of college, it is to a large extent mediated, enhanced, or counteracted by peer-group influence.

As college is a time in which change, growth, experimentation, and reconsideration is encouraged, it is also a time in which decisions are encouraged and precipitated. Personality is pretty well set in early childhood, but the later years of high school and of college are years in which a young person decides through considered choices or by default, where and how he or she will fit into society. There are decisions on curriculum, quality of endeavor, college, areas of concentration, career, friends, standards, values, interests, memberships, marriage, and so forth.

It is not surprising that while in college, students are responsive to the social issues of the day. This is a period of increased exposure to a larger world of knowledge, of widening opportunity, of meeting new people and having new experiences, and also a time when option-restricting decisions must be made. College tends to make one more liberal, less traditional, and more rationally consistent; but the focus of such socialization into society is on the issues that then confront society. Civil rights, war, poverty, and ecology are the issues of the present generation of students, and they show more sensitivity to these issues than their elders who went to college and were involved in social issues of their day.

Whether the changes of the college years continue into adult life and are strengthened or weakened seems to depend on the degree to which the changes are supported and reinforced by the perspectives and feelings of one's marriage partner, group of friends and associates, and the social status and roles the individual moves into as life goes by. Much of the impact of college — the time spent, the experience, the degree, and the entry into one's lifework — occurs not during that half decade or more, but over a lifetime of changing and evolving conditions. For instance, interests and media practices shift in college, but the years spent getting started in an occupation, in a family, and in buying a home are so preoccupying that it is not until about age 40 or 45 that a sharp increase occurs among the college educated in attention to news events. The college years, on the average, show little *change* in a student's amount of political information or participation, though this could be changing in recent years. Also, this finding may change with the advent of the vote for 18-year-olds. But in their adult years, college graduates more often than others inform themselves politically, turn out to vote, participate in campaigns, run successfully for political office, and care about political outcomes.

College also makes for a better life through a network of effects that become evident over the years. College graduates are situationally advantaged in monetary terms, but they also have better opportunities, more job security, and better working conditions. They report fewer job changes and higher job satisfaction. Their careers are better suited to meaningful and productive work in their later years. They are more confident and more optimistic about their own outlook and the national economy. Their jobs offer more fringe benefits; they save more and are more future-oriented; they plan more efficiently; take fewer risks in many areas (from health to insurance and use of seat belts).

College graduates are more likely to use the various resources and services of society. They belong to more organizations, are slightly more likely to go to church, and hold positions of leadership or expect to lead more frequently than those with less education. They are more introspective and concerned about personal and interpersonal aspects of life but relish more of the pleasures of interpersonal living. They have a greater sense of well-being. They tend to feel more socially efficacious and personally competent.

College graduates tend to be more supportive than others of protest but are not approving of obstructionist tactics. They support law and order but are not so approving as others of all-out use of force. The under-30 college graduates are strong supporters of civil rights, and most are less prejudiced in principle, and in a general sense, than those with less education. Prejudice against blacks seems to be little altered until one gets to the college educated on the education ladder. The prejudice of the college attender is less blatant and reflected in areas of more personal and intimate association.

On international involvements the college educated as a group are always better informed and more supportive than others. This includes support for peace ventures, alliances, and international organizations, as well as support for military ventures and military aid.

Education has increasingly become *the* bridge to better status. A person's status in society has traditionally been structured and defined by the characteristics of age, race, and sex, and the achieved characteristics of income, education, and occupation. Sex-defined status is under challenge, but educational achievement is one of the clearest bridges to happier marriage, a job, control of family size, and a feeling of meaningfulness. Race has been a barrier, but education is becoming *the* bridge to more equal status. Status associated with age is under challenge, spearheaded by the college-trained young.

Income, occupation, and education are related, but education is increasingly *the* key factor. Yet they are not interlocked. A teacher or nurse with a college education does not have a claim on a high income. A tool- and diemaker without a college education may have a significantly higher income. But a high-income business executive without college is becoming rare.

If all these six aspects of status tend to be equally high or low, sociologists speak of status consistency or status crystallization. But social structure is increasingly seen as a complex set of poorly intercorrelated hierarchies (Hughes, 1945; Jackson, 1962; Lenski, 1954). Age, race, and income, for instance, do not necessarily predict status. But educational achievement is so much a key factor that it can create a large amount of status consistency, reducing, but not yet eliminating, discrepancies of status related to race or sex, for example.

Educational attainment, however, can also create strains of status inconsistency. The black physician or lawyer is under some stress if not granted the income and prestige that are usually associated with that level of education and occupation. The college graduate expects many other characteristics to fall into line, and the reviewed data indicate that a number of characteristic differences are accrued. But it is interesting to note that liberal voting patterns are particularly associated with status inconsistency (Lenski, 1954), e.g., high education but not high prestige occupation or income. Trieman (1966) finds status inconsistency related to racial attitudes, and Rush (1967) to ultraconservative political attitudes. Increased educational attainment thus creates schisms and strains in the social network and reduces the influence of other differentials of status and class.

It is clear that the data are incomplete. Studies are needed to update findings in light of changing conditions. Studies are needed on the methodological problems of comparability of information from people with different levels of education. Projects need to focus on differences of institutions, programs, and students. Researchers need also to widen their scope to include social issues surrounding the college, the complex interactions of many variables, and the time-extended, life-cycle consequences of college. Although it is clear that a college of any kind has some significant social impact, higher education will better serve society if its patterns of influence and impact, success and failure, are better understood.

References

Adams, Bert N., and Miles T. Meidam: "Economics, Family Structure, and College Attendance," *American Journal of Sociology,* vol. 74, no. 3, pp. 230–239, The University of Chicago Press, Chicago, November 1968. © 1968 by the University of Chicago. All rights reserved.

Ahmed, Paul I.: "Family Hospital and Surgical Insurance Coverage," *Vital and Health Statistics,* ser. 10, no. 42, Washington, D.C., November 1967.

American Institute of Public Opinion: untitled release, Princeton, N.J., July 20, 1954.

Argyle, Michael: *Religious Behavior,* The Free Press, Glencoe, Ill., 1959.

Astin, Alexander W.: "College Impact on Student Attitudes and Behavior," speech delivered at the annual meeting of the American Association for the Advancement of Science, December 1970*a*.

Astin, Alexander W.: "Differential College Effects on the Motivation of Talented Students to Obtain the Ph.D.," *Journal of Educational Psychology,* vol. 54, no. 1, pp. 63–71, February 1963.

Astin, Alexander W.: "The Methodology of Research on College Impact, Part One," *Sociology of Education,* vol. 43, no. 3, pp. 223–254, Summer 1970*b*.

Astin, Alexander W.: " 'Productivity' of Undergraduate Institutions," *Science,* vol. 136, no. 3511, pp. 129–135, April 13, 1962.

Astin, Alexander W., and Robert J. Panos: *The Educational and Vocational Development of College Students,* American Council on Education, Washington, D.C., 1969.

Axelrod, Morris: "Urban Structure and Social Participation," *American Sociological Review,* vol. 21, no. 1, pp. 13–18, February 1956.

Barger, Ben, and Everette Hall: "The Interrelationships of Family Size and Socioeconomic Status for Parents of College Students," *Journal of Marriage and the Family,* vol. 28, no. 2, pp. 186–187, May 1966.

Bayer, Alan E.: "Birth Order and College Attendance," *Journal of Marriage and the Family,* vol. 28, no. 4, pp. 480–484, November 1966.

Bayley, Nancy, and Earl S. Schaefer: "Relationships between Socioeconomic Variables and Behavior of Mothers toward Young Children," *Journal of Genetic Psychology,* vol. 96, no. 1, pp. 61–77, March 1960.

Bidwell, Charles Everett, and Rebecca S. Vreeland: *Student Socialization in Harvard College: Path Analysis of College Impact* (forthcoming).

Blumenthal, Monica, Robert L. Kahn, and Frank M. Andrews: Personal communication, 1971.

Bogart, Leo: *The Age of Television,* Frederick Ungar Publishing Co., New York, 1958.

Bogart, Leo: "ANPA Study of TV Advertising," unpublished, 1967.

Boland, Walter R.: "Size, Organization, and Environmental Mediation: A Study of Colleges and Universities," in Wolf Heydebrand (ed.), *Comparative Organizations: The Results of Empirical Research,* Prentice-Hall, Inc., Englewood Cliffs, N.J., 1971.

Bowman, Mary Jean: "The Land Grant Colleges and Universities in Human Resource Development," *Journal of Economic History,* vol. 22, no. 4, pp. 523–546, December 1962.

Brim, Orville G., Jr.: "Socialization through the Life Cycle," in Orville G. Brim, Jr., and Stanton Wheeler (eds.), *Socialization after Childhood,* John Wiley & Sons, Inc., New York, 1966.

Brim, Orville G., Jr., David Glass, John Neulinger, and Ira Firestone: *American Beliefs and Attitudes about Intelligence,* Russell Sage Foundation, New York, 1969.

Brown, Donald R., and Lois-Ellin Datta: "Authoritarianism, Verbal Ability, and Response Set," *Journal of Abnormal and Social Psychology,* vol. 58, no. 1, pp. 131–134, January 1959.

Brown, Robert D.: "Manipulation of the Environmental Press in a College Residence Hall," *Personnel and Guidance Journal,* vol. 46, no. 6, pp. 555–560, February 1968.

Campbell, Angus: "Factors Associated with Attitudes toward Jews," in Theodore M. Newcomb and Eugene L. Hartley (eds.), *Readings in Social Psychology,* Henry Holt and Company, Inc., New York, 1947.

Campbell, Angus: Personal communication, 1971.

Campbell, Angus, Philip Converse, Warren Miller, and Donald Stokes: *The American Voter,* John Wiley & Sons, Inc., New York, 1960.

Campbell, Angus, and William C. Eckerman: *Public Concepts of the Value and Cost of Higher Education,* Institute for Social Research, The University of Michigan, Ann Arbor, 1964.

Campbell, Angus, and Howard Schuman: "Racial Attitudes in Fifteen American Cities," in *Supplemental Studies for the National Advisory Commission on Civil Disorders,* U.S. Government · Printing Office, Washington, D.C., 1968.

Cannell, Charles F., Gordon Fisher, and Thomas Bakker: "Reporting of Hospitalization," *Vital and Health Statistics,* ser. D, no. 4, Washington, D.C., 1961.

Cannell, Charles F., Floyd Fowler, and Kent Marquis: "The Influence of Interviewer and Respondent Psychological and Behavioral Variables on the Reporting in Household Interviews," *Vital and Health Statistics,* ser, 2, no. 26, Washington, D.C., March 1968.

Cannell, Charles F., and James MacDonald: "The Impact of Health News on Attitudes and Behavior," *Journalism Quarterly,* vol. 33, no. 3, pp. 315–323, Summer 1956.

Cass, James, and Max Birnbaum (eds.): *Comparative Guide to American Colleges,* Harper & Row, Publishers, Incorporated, New York, 1964.

Chickering, Arthur W.: "The Best Colleges Have the Least Effect," *Saturday Review,* vol. 54, no. 3, pp. 48–50, 54, January 16, 1971.

Chickering, Arthur W.: "College Experience and Student Development," speech given at the meeting of the American Association for the Advancement of Science, 1970.

Clark, Burton R.: "The 'Cooling-Out' Function in Higher Education," *American Journal of Sociology,* vol. 65, no. 6, pp. 569–576, May 1960.

Converse, Philip E.: "Change in the American Electorate," in Angus Campbell and Philip E. Converse (eds.), *The Human Meaning of Social Change* (forthcoming).

Converse, Philip E.: "Of Time and Partisan Stability," *Comparative Political Studies,* vol. 2, no. 2, pp. 139–171, July 1969.

Converse, Philip E., and Howard Schuman: "'Silent Majorities' and the Vietnam War," *Scientific American,* vol. 222, no. 6, pp. 17–25, June 1970. Copyright © 1970 by Scientific American, Inc. All rights reserved.

Cremin, Lawrence A.: "Horace Mann's Legacy," in Lawrence A. Cremin (ed.), *Horace Mann, The Republic and the School,* Bureau of Publication, Teachers College, Columbia University, New York, 1957.

Davis, James A.: *Great Aspirations: The Graduate School Plans of America's College Seniors,* Aldine Publishing Co., Chicago, 1964.

Davis, Robert C.: *The Public Impact of Science in the Mass Media,* Institute for Social Research, The University of Michigan, Ann Arbor, 1958.

Deutsch, Steven E.: "The Impact of Cross-Cultural Relations on the Campus," *Sociology and Social Research,* vol. 53, no. 2, pp. 137–146, January 1969.

Douvan, Elizabeth (Malcolm), and Alan M. Walker: "The Sense of Effectiveness in Public Affairs," *Psychological Monographs: General and Applied,* vol. 70, no. 22, pp. 1–19, 1956.

Dunn, James P., George Brooks, Judith Mausner, Gerald P. Rodnan, and Sidney Cobb: "Social Class Gradient of Serum Uric Acid Levels in Males," *Journal of the American Medical Association,* vol. 185, pp. 431–436, August 10, 1963.

Dupuy, Harold J., Arnold Engel, Brian K. Devine, James Scanlon, and Linda Querec: "Selected Symptoms of Psychological Distress," *Vital and Health Statistics,* ser. 11, no. 37, Washington, D.C., August 1970.

Elder, Glen H., Jr.: *Adolescent Achievement and Mobility Aspirations,* Institute for Research in Social Science, Chapel Hill, N.C., 1962.

Ellis, Robert A., and W. Clayton Lane: "Structural Supports for Upward Mobility," *American Sociological Review,* vol. 28, no. 5, pp. 743–756, October 1963.

Feldman, Kenneth A.: "Measuring College Environments: Some Uses of Path Analysis," *American Educational Research Journal,* vol. 8, no. 1, January 1971.

Feldman, Kenneth A.: "Studying the Impacts of Colleges on Students," *Sociology of Education,* vol. 42, no. 3, pp. 207–237, Summer 1969.

Feldman, Kenneth A., and Theodore M. Newcomb: *The Impact of College on Students,* vols. I and II, Jossey-Bass, San Francisco, Calif., 1969.

Finney, Henry Christopher: "Development and Change of Political Libertarianism among Berkeley Undergraduates," unpublished doctoral dissertation, University of California, Berkeley, 1967.

Fisher, Burton, and Stephen Withey: *Big Business as the People See It,* Institute for Social Research, The University of Michigan, Ann Arbor, 1951.

Flacks, Richard: "The Liberated Generation: An Exploration of the Roots of Student Protest," *Journal of Social Issues,* vol. 23, no. 3, pp. 52–75, July 1967.

Flanagan, John Clemens, and William W. Cooley: *Project Talent: One Year Follow-Up Studies,* University of Pittsburgh, Pittsburgh, Pa., 1966.

Folger, John K., Helen S. Astin, and Alan E. Bayer: *Human Resources and Higher Education,* Staff Report of the Commission on Human Resources and Advanced Education, Russell Sage Foundation, New York, 1969.

Fowler, Floyd Jackson, Jr.: "Education, Interaction, and Interview Performance," dissertation, The University of Michigan, 1965.

Freedman, Mervin B.: *The College Experience,* Jossey-Bass, San Francisco, Calif., 1967.

Freedman, Mervin B., and Carl Bereiter: "A Longitudinal Study of Personality Development in College Alumnae," *Merrill-Palmer Quarterly of Behavior and Development,* vol. 9, no. 4, pp. 295–301, October 1963.

Freedman, Ronald, Pascal K. Whelpton, and Arthur A. Campbell: *Family Planning, Sterility and Population Growth,* McGraw-Hill Book Company, New York, 1959.

Gamson, Zelda F.: "Utilitarian and Normative Orientations toward Education," *Sociology of Education,* vol. 39, no. 1, pp. 46–73, Winter 1966.

Glock, Charles Y., Benjamin Ringer, and Earl Babbie: *To Comfort and to Challenge,* University of California Press, Berkeley, Calif., 1967.

Gurin, Gerald, Joseph Veroff, and Sheila Feld: *Americans View Their Mental Health,* Basic Books, Inc., New York, 1960. © 1960 by Basic Books, Inc., Publishers, New York.

Harris, Chester William (ed.): *Problems in Measuring Change,* The University of Wisconsin Press, Madison, 1963.

Head, Kendra: "On College Education," working memo 51, Institute for Social Research, The University of Michigan, Ann Arbor, June 1970. (Mimeographed.)

Hofstadter, Richard: *Anti-Intellectualism in American Life,* Alfred A. Knopf, Inc., New York, 1963.

Houthakker, Hendrik S.: "Education and Income," *The Review of Economics and Statistics,* vol. 41, no. 1, pp. 24–28, February 1959.

Hughes, Everett Cherrington: "Dilemmas and Contradictions of Status," *American Journal of Sociology,* vol. 50, no. 5, pp. 353–359, March 1945.

Jackson, Elton F.: "Status Consistency and Symptoms of Stress," *American Sociological Review,* vol. 27, no. 4, pp. 469–480, August 1962.

Jacob, Philip E.: *Changing Values in College: An Exploratory Study of the Impact of College Teaching,* Harper & Row, Publishers, Incorporated, New York, 1957.

Jaffe, Abram J., and Walter Adams: *American Higher Education in Transition,* Bureau of Applied Social Research, Columbia University, New York, 1969. (Mimeographed.)

Jencks, Christopher, and David Reisman: *The Academic Revolution,* Doubleday & Company, Inc., Garden City, N.Y., 1968.

Kagan, Jerome, and Marion Freeman: "Relation of Childhood Intelligence, Maternal Behaviors and Social Class to Behavior during Adolescence," *Child Development,* vol. 34, no. 4, pp. 899–911, December 1963.

Kagan, Jerome, and Howard A. Moss: *Birth to Maturity: A Study in Psychological Development,* John Wiley & Sons, Inc., New York, 1962.

Katona, George, William Dunkelberg, Gary Hendricks, and Jay Schmiedeskamp: *1969 Survey of Consumer Finances,* Institute for Social Research, The University of Michigan, Ann Arbor, 1970.

Katona, George, Burkhard Strumpel, and Ernest Zahn: *Aspirations and Affluence,* McGraw-Hill Book Company, New York, 1971.

Katz, Joseph: *No Time for Youth: Growth and Constraint in College Students,* Jossey-Bass, San Francisco, Calif., 1968.

Keller, Suzanne: *Beyond the Ruling Class,* Random House, Inc., New York, 1963.

Korn, Harold A.: "Personality Scale Changes from the Freshman Year to the Senior Year," in Joseph Katz (ed.), *No Time for Youth: Growth and Constraint in College Students,* Jossey-Bass, San Francisco, Calif., 1968.

Krauss, Irving: "Sources of Educational Aspriations among Working-Class Youth," *American Sociological Review,* vol. 28, no. 6, pp. 867–879, December 1964.

Lansing, John, Gerald Ginsburg, and Kaisa Braaten: *An Investigation of Response Error,* Bureau of Economic and Business Research, University of Illinois, Urbana, 1961.

Lavin, David E.: *The Prediction of Academic Performance,* Russell Sage Foundation, New York, 1965.

Lazarsfeld, Paul: *The People Look at Radio,* The University of North Carolina Press, Chapel Hill, 1946.

Lenski, Gerhard E.: *The Religious Factor,* Doubleday & Company, Inc., Garden City, N.Y., 1961.

Lenski, Gerhard E.: "Status Crystallization: A Non-Vertical Dimension of Social Status," *American Sociological Review,* vol. 19, no. 4, pp. 405–413, August 1954.

McClintock, Charles G., and Henry A. Turner: "The Impact of College upon Political Knowledge, Participation and Values," *Human Relations,* vol. 15, no. 2, pp. 163–176, May 1962.

Matthews, Donald: *The Social Background of Political Decision-Makers,* Doubleday & Company, Inc., Garden City, N.Y., 1954.

Metzner, Charles: *Interest, Information and Attitudes in the Field of World Affairs,* Institute for Social Research, The University of Michigan, Ann Arbor, 1949.

Michael, John A.: "High School Climates and Plans for Entering College," *Public Opinion Quarterly,* vol. 25, no. 4, pp. 585–595, Winter 1961.

Miller, Neal Elgar: "Academic Climate and Student Values," paper read at the 54th annual meeting of the American Sociological Association, 1959.

Morgan, James N.: "Contributions of Survey Research to Economics," in Charles Y. Glock (ed.), *Survey Research in the Social Sciences,* Russell Sage Foundation, New York, 1967.

Morgan, James N., and Martin H. David: "Education and Income," *Quarterly Journal of Economics,* vol. 77, no. 3, pp. 423–437, August 1963.

Morgan, James N., Martin H. David, Wilbur J. Cohen, and Harvey E. Brazer: *Income and Welfare in the United States,* McGraw-Hill Book Company, New York, 1962.

Morgan, James N., and Charles Lininger: "Education and Income: Comment," *Quarterly Journal of Economics,* vol. 78, no. 2, pp. 346–347, May 1964.

Morgan, James N., and Ismail A. Sirageldin: "A Note on the Quality Dimension in Education," *Journal of Political Economy,* vol. 76, no. 5, pp. 1069–1077, September/October 1968.

Morgan, James N., Ismail A. Sirageldin, and Nancy Baerwaldt: *Productive Americans, A Study of How Individuals Contribute to Economic Progress,* Institute for Social Research, The University of Michigan, Ann Arbor, 1966.

Mueller, Eva (with Judith Hybels, Jay Schmiedeskamp, John Sonquist, and Charles Staelin): *Technological Advance in an Expanding Economy: Its Impact on a Cross-Section of the Labor Force,* Institute for Social Research, The University of Michigan, Ann Arbor, 1969.

National Opinion Research Center (NORC): *Cincinnati Looks at the United Nations,* report no. 37, The University of Chicago Press, Chicago, 1947.

Nelson, Erland N. P.: "Patterns of Religious Attitude Shifts from College to Fourteen Years Later," *Psychological Monographs: General and Applied,* vol. 70, no. 6, pp. 1–22, 1956.

Nelson, Erland N. P.: "Radicalism-Conservatism in Student Attitudes," *Psychological Monographs,* vol. 50, no. 4, pp. 1–31, 1938.

Newcomb, Theodore M.: *Personality and Social Change: Attitude Formation in a Student Community,* Holt, Rinehart and Winston, Inc., New York, 1943.

Newcomb, Theodore, Donald R. Brown, James A. Kulik, William R. Revelle, and David J. Reimer: "Self-Selection and Change," in Jerry G. Gaff (ed.), *The Cluster College,* Jossey-Bass, San Francisco, 1970.

Newcomb, Theodore M., Kathryn E. Koenig, Richard Flacks, and Donald P. Warwick: *Persistence and Change: Bennington College and Its Students after Twenty-Five Years,* John Wiley & Sons, Inc., New York, 1967.

Pace, Charles Robert: *College and University Environment Scales (second edition): Technical Manual,* Educational Testing Service, Princeton, N.J., 1969 (first edition, 1963).

Pace, Charles Robert, and George G. Stern: "An Approach to the Measurement of Psychological Characteristics of College Environments," *Journal of Educational Psychology,* vol. 49, no. 5, pp. 269–277, October 1958.

Plant, Walter T.: "Longitudinal Changes in Intolerance and Authoritarianism for Subjects Differing in Amount of College Education over Four Years," *Genetic Psychology Monographs,* vol. 72, no. 2, pp. 247–287, November 1965.

Plant, Walter T.: "Personality Changes Associated with a College Education," U.S. Dept. HEW Cooperative Research Branch Project 348 (SAE 7666), San Jose State College, San Jose, Calif., 1962.

Prewitt, Kenneth: *The Recruitment of Political Leaders: A Study of Citizen-Politicians,* Bobbs-Merrill Co., Inc., New York, 1970.

Robinson, John P.: *Public Information about World Affairs,* Institute for Social Research, The University of Michigan, Ann Arbor, 1967.

Robinson, John P., and Philip E. Converse: *Summary of American Time Use Survey,* Institute for Social Research, The University of Michigan, Ann Arbor, 1966.

Robinson, John P., and Philip E. Converse: "The Impact of Television on Mass Media Usage: A Cross-national Comparison," *Transactions of the Sixth World Congress of Sociology,* vol. 3, International Sociological Association, 1970.

Rosen, Bernard C.: "Race, Ethnicity, and the Achievement Syndrome," *American Sociological Review,* vol. 24, no. 1, pp. 47–60, February 1959.

Rush, Gary B.: "Status Consistency and Right-Wing Extremism," *American Sociological Review,* vol. 32, no. 1, pp. 86–92, February 1967.

Ryder, Norman B., and Charles F. Westoff: "Relationships among Intended, Expected, Desired and Ideal Family Size: United States 1965," *Population Research,* March 1969.

Schacter, Stanley: "Birth Order, Eminence, and Higher Education," *American Sociological Review,* vol. 28, no. 5, pp. 757–768, October 1963.

Schuman, Howard, and John Harding: "Prejudice and the Norm of Rationality," *Sociometry,* vol. 27, no. 3, pp. 353–371, September 1964.

Scott, William A., and Stephen B. Withey: *The United States and the United Nations: The Public View, 1945–1955,* Manhattan Publishing Co., New York, 1958.

Selvin, Hanan C., and Warren O. Hagstrom: "Determinants of Support for Civil Liberties," *British Journal of Sociology,* vol. 11, no. 1, pp. 51–73, March 1960.

Sewell, William H.: "Community of Residence and College Plans," *American Sociological Review,* vol. 29, no. 1, pp. 24–38, February 1964.

Sewell, William H., and J. Michael Armer: "Neighborhood Context and College Plans," *American Sociological Review,* vol. 31, no. 2, pp. 159–168, April 1966.

Sewell, William H., Archibald O. Haller, and Murray A. Straus: "Social Status and Educational and Occupational Aspiration," *American Sociological Review,* vol. 22, no. 1, pp. 67–73, February 1957.

Sewell, William H., and Vimal P. Shah: "Parents' Education and Children's Educational Aspirations and Achievements," *American Sociological Review,* vol. 33, no. 2, pp. 191–209, April 1968*a.*

Sewell, William H., and Vimal P. Shah: "Social Class, Parental Encouragement, and Educational Aspirations," *American Journal of Sociology,* vol. 73, no. 5, pp. 559–572, The University of Chicago Press, Chicago, March 1968*b*. © 1968 by the University of Chicago. All rights reserved.

Sewell, William H., and Vimal P. Shah: "Socioeconomic Status, Intelligence, and the Attainment of Higher Education," *Sociology of Education,* vol. 40, no. 1, pp. 1–23, Winter 1967.

Siegel, Alberta Engvall, and Sidney Siegel: "Reference Groups, Membership Groups, and Attitude Change," *Journal of Abnormal and Social Psychology,* vol. 55, no. 3, pp. 360–364, November 1957.

Simmons, W. R., and Staff: *Selective Markets and the Media Reaching Them: 1969 Comprehensive Television Audience Report,* W. R. Simmons and Associates Research, Inc., New York, 1969.

Spady, William G.: "Educational Mobility and Access: Growth and Paradoxes," *American Journal of Sociology,* vol. 73, no. 3, pp. 273–286, The University of Chicago Press, Chicago, November 1967. © 1967 by the University of Chicago. All rights reserved.

Spaeth, Joe L., and Norman Miller: "Trends in the Career Plans and Activities of June, 1961, College Graduates," National Opinion Research Center, Chicago, 1965.

Stafford, Frank: "A Note on Recent Trends in Income Inequality," unpublished.

Starch, D., and Staff: *35th Annual Media Study of Primary Audiences; Consumption of Media,* Daniel Starch and Staff, Inc., New York, 1969.

Steiner, Gary A.: *The People Look at Television,* Alfred A. Knopf, Inc., New York, 1963.

Stember, Charles H.: *Education and Attitude Change: The Effect of Schooling on Prejudice against Minority Groups,* Institute of Human Relations Press, New York, 1961.

Stern, George G.: *People in Context: Measuring Person-Environment Congruence in Education and Industry,* John Wiley & Sons, Inc., New York, 1970.

Stouffer, Samuel: *Communism, Conformity and Civil Liberties,* Doubleday & Company, Inc., Garden City, New York, 1955.

Strong, Edward Kellogg: *Vocational Interests 18 Years after College,* The University of Minnesota Press, Minneapolis, 1955.

Survey Research Center: *America's Role in World Affairs, Patterns of Citizen Opinion, 1949–1950,* Institute for Social Research, The University of Michigan, Ann Arbor, 1952.

Survey Research Center: *Attitudes toward United States-Russian Relations, October, 1948. A National Survey,* Institute for Social Research, The University of Michigan, Ann Arbor, 1948.

Survey Research Center: *Public Attitudes toward American Foreign Policy, A Nation-wide Survey,* part II of *Attitudes toward the Major Issues of Foreign Policy,* Institute for Social Research, The University of Michigan, Ann Arbor, 1947.

Telford, Charles Witt, and Walter T. Plant: "The Psychological Impact of the Public Two-Year College on Certain Non-intellectual Functions," U.S. Dept. HEW Cooperative Research Branch Project SAE 8646, San Jose State College, San Jose, Calif., 1963.

Tichenor, Philip J., George A. Donohue, and Clarice N. Olien: "Mass Media Flow and Differential Growth in Knowledge," *Public Opinion Quarterly,* vol. 34, no. 2, pp. 159–170, Summer 1970.

Trent, James W., and Leland L. Medsker: *Beyond High School,* Jossey-Bass, San Francisco, Calif., 1968.

Trieman, Donald J.: "Status Discrepancy and Prejudice," *American Journal of Sociology,* vol. 71, no. 6, pp. 651–664, May 1966.

Trow, Martin: "Education and Survey Research," in Charles Y. Glock (ed.), *Survey Research in the Social Sciences,* Russell Sage Foundation, New York, 1967.

U.S. Bureau of the Census: *Current Population Reports,* ser. P-60, no. 74, "Annual Mean Income, Lifetime Income, and Educational Attainment of Men in the United States, for Selected Years, 1956–1968," Washington, D.C., 1970.

U.S. Bureau of the Census: *Historical Statistics of the United States, Colonial Times to 1957,* Washington, D.C., 1960.

U.S. Bureau of the Census: *Historical Statistics of the United States, Continuation to 1962 and Revisions,* Washington, D.C., 1965.

U.S. Dept. of Commerce, Bureau of the Census: ser. P-20, no. 183, May 22, 1969; no. 185, July 11, 1969; no. 194, Feb. 19, 1970; and no. 204, July 13, 1970.

U.S. Department of Labor: *Manpower Report of the President,* Washington, D.C., April 1968.

Vreeland, Rebecca S., and Charles E. Bidwell: "Classifying University Departments: An Approach to the Analysis of Their Effects upon Undergraduates' Values and Attitudes," *Sociology of Education,* vol. 39, no. 3, pp. 237–254, Summer 1966.

Vreeland, Rebecca S., and Charles E. Bidwell: "Organizational Effects on Student Attitudes: A Study of the Harvard Houses," *Sociology of Education,* vol. 38, no. 3, pp. 233–250, Spring 1965.

Wallace, Walter L.: *Student Culture: Social Structure and Continuity in a Liberal Arts College,* Aldine Publishing Company, Chicago, 1966.

Weiss, Carol: *Validity of Interview Responses of Welfare Mothers,* Bureau of Applied Social Research, Columbia University, New York, 1968.

Werts, Charles E.: "Path Analysis: Testimonial of a Proselyte," *American Journal of Sociology,* vol. 73, no. 4, pp. 509–512, January 1968.

Westoff, Charles F., and Norman B. Ryder: "Experience with Oral Contraceptives in the U.S., 1960–65," *Clinical Obstetrics & Gynecology,* vol. 11, no. 3, pp. 734–752, September 1968.

Whelpton, Pascal K., Arthur A. Campbell, and John E. Patterson: *Fertility and Family Planning in the United States,* Princeton University Press, Princeton, N.J., 1966.

Wilder, Charles S.: "Family Health Expenses," *Vital and Health Statistics,* ser. 10, no. 41, Washington, D.C., November 1967.

Wilder, Charles S.: "Family Use of Health Services," *Vital and Health Statistics,* ser. 10, no. 55, Washington, D.C., July 1969.

Wilensky, Harold L.: "Mass Society and Mass Culture," *American Sociological Review,* vol. 29, no. 2, pp. 173–197, April 1964.

Withey, Stephen B.: *Fourth Survey of Public Knowledge and Attitudes Concerning Civil Defense,* Institute for Social Research, The University of Michigan, Ann Arbor, 1954.

Wright, Charles, and Herbert Hyman: "Social Influences upon the Membership," in William Glaser and David Sills (eds.), *The Government of Associations,* Bedminster Press, Totowa, N.J., 1966.

Yearbook of Labor Statistics, International Labor Office, Geneva, Switzerland, various years.

Index

*This book was set in Vladimir by University Graphics, Inc.
It was printed on acid-free, long-life paper and bound by
The Maple Press Company. The designers were Elliot Epstein
and Edward Butler. The editors were Herbert Waentig and Cheryl
Allen for McGraw-Hill Book Company and Verne A. Stadtman and
Dennis Wynn for the Carnegie Commission on Higher Education.
Frank Matonti and Alice Cohen supervised the production.*